DISCARD

The Gardens of
Luciano Giubbilei

Andrew Wilson
Photography by Steven Wooster

The Gardens of
Luciano Giubbilei

Foreword by Tom Stuart-Smith

MERRELL
LONDON · NEW YORK

In memory of my grandmother

Foreword
Tom Stuart-Smith

I first encountered Luciano Giubbilei about ten years ago. I was working on a garden in west London and happened to peep through the hedge into the neighbouring plot, an impeccable, streamlined garden of limestone paths, immaculately clipped pleached trees and a quiet aura of calm and poise. Quite a contrast to the mass of compost and half-finished chaos that surrounded me. There was nothing flashy about it; instead it was pervaded by a beautifully serene and restful confidence.

Since then I have seen more of Luciano's work in publication and in the flesh, and there is a pleasing and seemingly effortless consistency to it. As a fellow practitioner, I know how extraordinarily difficult it is to achieve the understated, as it requires not only clarity of vision but also very gritty persistence. What may seem simple on the surface is often absurdly complex underneath, and one small element out of place can wreck the entire vision.

Most of the gardens featured in this book are outdoor rooms, extensions of internal living space for people who love the idea of the garden but are not gardeners. They are in the great tradition of Le Nôtre's *jardins de verdure*, where plants provided the theatrical and architectural backdrop for court ceremony and extravagant sculpture. In Luciano's case there is a modest, Modernist understatement, and the spaces rely rather on their beautiful proportions, exquisitely detailed finishes and a more subtle use of sculpture and furniture for their animation.

The gardens are like the man, impeccably turned out, suave and urbane in a gentle way, quietly assertive but never bossy. Sophisticated and thoroughly Italian. It's a style I admire partly because I know I could never do it as well. It provides a form of instant theatre, where the designer forges places, conjures atmosphere and creates spaces out of nothing. This is a great art, and one that is illustrated masterfully in this beautiful book.

I have always
wanted to write a
book about light.
I can think of
nothing that
reminds me more of
eternity; my mind
is relaxed observing
the play of light.

Preface
Luciano Giubbilei

As I reflect on my career, from my early fascination with photography, Classical gardens, interior design, architecture and contemporary art, to my more recent interest in the aesthetic beauty of nature blended with human intervention, a comment by John Sales (former gardens adviser at the National Trust, quoted by Eric Haskell in *Le Nôtre's Gardens*, 1997) comes to mind:

> Gardening is to a large degree performance art, and like all great music and theatre, gardens need to be constantly reinterpreted to retain their relevance and vitality, while preserving the original fabric.

Designing gardens is truly a process of discovery. For me, it is not just about making a garden, but also about making a comment on life and on the qualities that are important to me. My gardens are a reflection of the way I live; I cannot separate them from that. London has been particularly influential in the way I design and in the person that I am today. I remember very clearly the empowering energy I felt when I first arrived, walking through the streets and feeling that anything was possible. I still feel it today.

This book illustrates a particular period of my work, rather than attempting to be a definite representation of a set style. I have never wanted to make a book exclusively about me, or even about my work, because I share my projects with a great number of collaborators – nursery owners, craftsmen, contractors and artists – all of whom inspire me by sharing their knowledge and talents. Chapters in this book explain in greater detail how they help me to realize my vision.

It is my belief that the greatest contribution I can make as a designer is to link the human and the natural so as to evoke my place in the wider world. For this reason, rather than being purely decorative, my work concerns the articulation of space.

I hope this book will give you an insight into what we do as garden designers, and more specifically into the way I create my gardens. It illustrates twelve projects, which are individually designed for the people who live with these spaces. I never work alone, since I relish the immediate, dynamic exchange with my clients, who have chosen me to realize our common idea of how to live. They give me input and encouragement, and that is why each garden I create is unique.

I could not remain constantly inspired and enthusiastic without Sarah, who has supported me and believed in me for the last twenty years. This book is for her.

Introduction

Balthazar Korab's evocative photographs of the Villa Gamberaia (previous pages) effectively set Luciano on the path he has followed now for nearly twenty years. The Via Giovanni Dupré in Siena (below) is where Luciano lived with his grandmother. Sun-drenched walls and faceted rooftops glow against deep shadows in the narrow confines of the city's streets.

Sitting in the cool, shaded interior of Luciano Giubbilei's London apartment, I am struck by the expanses of dark polished wood combined with the neutral tones of the walls and furnishings. Light filters in through louvred half-shutters, revealing the blue sky and tall plane trees in the square beyond; we listen to Beethoven as we chat. Characteristic of the man and his approach to life both as a designer and as a human being, the room exudes the quiet confidence of the gardens for which he is well known.

Luciano was born and raised in the Tuscan town of Siena, where he lived with his grandmother during the school terms. With her simple existence of focused routines centred on her grandson, she would have a formative influence on Luciano's life and design philosophy. He would watch her meticulously preparing food, always with the best ingredients despite her modest pension. That love of food and of the simple processes of cooking and sharing has remained with him and is embodied in the social spaces in the gardens he creates.

The ancient, tightly packed city was for Luciano and his friends a playground of narrow passages and densely layered architecture. From it, he feels, come his spatial thinking – defined in particular by the mass of planting – and his fascination with the play of intense sunlight and deep shadow.

On leaving school Luciano was unsure about his future, and began, but did not finish, a three-year course in preparation for a secure career with a leading bank of Siena. At eighteen a year of National Service in northern Italy broke the link with home, and, once back in civilian life, he found a job delivering pastries across Tuscany. That remains a favourite time in his life. Inspired by the beauty of the landscape, he would photograph the way the light changed, the views or details of materials, architecture and planting with a growing sense of excitement and enthusiasm.

At this time Luciano met Sarah, a young English woman living in Italy to learn the language. Her relaxed and easy confidence was noticeably different from the liveliness and intensity of the local people, a contrast that Luciano enjoyed. More importantly, his growing sense of commitment to their relationship made him think more seriously about the future.

Living with Sarah in the heart of the Tuscan countryside at the edge of a vineyard, Luciano became increasingly interested in the management of the vines and of a small vegetable garden that he set up with the help of the vineyard manager. His fascination lay in the realization that the landscape was a combined effort between man and nature, and that the order and repetition of the vine rows corrugating the hillsides played against the undulating topography of meadows and copses in a theatrical way. Luciano admired the dedication and care of the men working in the fields, noting their passion for and application of knowledge. He also loved nurturing, cooking and eating his own produce, enjoying the raw connection to the land.

With a growing sense that this was what he had been searching for, Luciano turned first to horticulture, visiting the gardens of Tuscany for inspiration and in the hope of finding work. He had neither experience nor formal qualifications, but intended to offer his help, hoping to learn from the master gardeners he met.

Arriving early one morning at Villa Gamberaia, the celebrated seventeenth-century garden near Florence, Luciano was staggered by the view of the house from the gate. The head gardener, Silvano, who had worked there since the end of the Second World War, shouted from the terrace that the villa was closed, but Luciano persisted. Silvano could not pay him, but agreed that Luciano could work with him, clipping and clearing as the seasons changed. A passionate man, Silvano was dedicated to his family and to the garden, which represented a lifetime of unstinting care and dedication.

They enjoyed talking and sharing ideas, and after their third meeting Silvano offered Luciano a paid position. Luciano considered accepting, but realized that he needed to go to college. The focus of his life had changed: a passion for gardens was growing within him, and he knew it was garden design that now beckoned.

When Luciano left Gamberaia, Silvano presented him with a black-and-white photographic record of the garden, a book that would prove a significant influence once his design career was under way. The atmospheric photographs by Balthazar Korab depicted both the architecture and the mood of the garden: deep, rich shadows played on intensely lit surfaces, their textures almost tangible.

Luciano investigated Florence's botanical school and looked into studying landscape architecture, but somehow both seemed divorced from the making of gardens. In 1993 he and Sarah decided to travel to London for a holiday, during which Luciano would visit some of the colleges there. Luciano came to the Inchbald School of Design in London for an interview with me and to visit the summer exhibition of students' work. He knew immediately that this was the place for him, sensing the enthusiasm of the students, who, inspired by their studies, were producing exciting designs. Spurred on by this prospect, in January 1994 he left Italy for England with Sarah, first to study English and then to start his course in garden design.

Luciano excelled at Inchbald, soaking up every minute of studio tuition and constantly asking questions. Always the last to leave each day, he spent as much time as possible researching and developing ideas and discussing them in depth with me. His three watchwords now are 'process', 'passion' and 'learning', and those are certainly qualities I detected in him during our studio sessions. He was fascinated and stimulated, but it was a fragile experience; returning to Siena for six weeks after graduation, he could feel the energy he had experienced in London diminishing, perhaps replaced by his fondness for home.

The contrast between the two aspects of Luciano's life – the ancient sun-drenched stones of Siena and the grey immensity of London – was marked, and he found the new city alien at first. Yet garden design was thriving there, especially at that time. The first television programme dedicated to garden design rather than horticulture had been broadcast in 1989 (David Stevens's *Gardens by Design*), and, as the British economy started to move out of recession in the early 1990s, the relatively young profession of the garden designer started to expand dramatically. The property market was also increasing, and – as a direct result – the demand for new and refurbished private gardens soared. Luciano had taken the right step at the right time. He knew the future lay in London, a bustling city with a climate and client base that matched few places on Earth, and came to love its rich culture and its diversity of life and architecture. Art and design were enjoying a new sense of direction in the city, creating a buzz and optimism that Luciano wanted to be part of. London has been as important to him both personally and professionally as Siena; for his gardens, it was an essential catalyst.

In 1995, at the autumn conference of the Society of Garden Designers, Luciano met the garden designer Anthony Paul, who lectures at Inchbald and who had taken him with other students to The Netherlands for a meeting with the designer and plantsman Piet Oudolf, then relatively unknown in the UK. For eighteen months Luciano worked with and learned from Paul in the beautiful setting of his studio and garden in Ockley, Surrey, starting to develop his own style and approach.

In 1996 Luciano decided to start his own business, part of which was providing flowers for Giorgio Locatelli's elegant London restaurant. The floristry provided an income and, more importantly, allowed him to make connections with people who could

use his skills as a garden designer. In Belgravia he discovered a wider client base, many of whom refreshed their gardens seasonally with new planting or furniture, pots and containers. He found that he worked well with and was inspired by the architects and interior designers who also served this community, and they would often recommend him to their clients.

In 1997, as he planted a scheme for a new restaurant, a passer-by who liked his style invited him to create what Luciano describes as his breakthrough garden, for her house in Harcourt Terrace (opposite). It remains a signature scheme, and forms a bridge to the gardens we now see as essentially those of Luciano Giubbilei.

The client, who is Danish, had strong views about gardens that chimed with Luciano's own. Her garden is a decked roof terrace accessed by wide doors from the conservatory and dining room. She had designed her own interiors, but needed help in the garden, which was uncharted territory for her. Luciano, excited to have found a client keen to invest in his ideas, perceived her careful attention to detail and love of fine objects, and explored the similarity in their approaches to design in his development of the garden. The client became intimately involved, engaging her own builder to render the terrace walls. The ritual of enjoying good food, so crucial to Luciano, was embodied in the development of the garden and in its connection to the dining room. Outdoor entertainment and social connection are important in all his schemes, and he creates spaces influenced by architecture and interior design rather than by gardening and horticulture. Although the finished garden closely followed the client's design thinking, it was the first time Luciano's philosophy had been enshrined in a garden, and represented a significant milestone for him.

The deck was bleached to provide a neutral surface for the rest of the design. Maples (*Acer palmatum* 'Dissectum Purpureum') were placed in slatted oak containers by Philippe Hurel, and cushions of box (*Buxus*

Three definitive views
of the Harcourt Terrace
garden illustrate its precise
geometry and fusion with
the supporting interiors.
They also illustrate the
importance of photography
to the designer of private
gardens, whose work would
otherwise be known only
by clients and their friends.

Andy Goldsworthy's installation *Stone Room* at the Yorkshire Sculpture Park (2007; top) explores forms similar to those in Luciano's roof garden in Geneva.

Leaf Stalk Room (2007; above), also by Goldsworthy at Yorkshire Sculpture Park, is atmospheric, with veils of light and silhouettes.

sempervirens) in funnel-shaped biscuitware pots from Kent as a break from the more typical terracotta. Chinese jars ornamented limestone plinths on either side of the seats. The focus was the furniture: a set of armchairs and a low table by American manufacturer Sutherland. It remains out of doors all year, creating a true outdoor room that can be used at virtually any time in London's equable climate. The furniture – sourced with the help of his client – has become something of a signature for Luciano. He wished to avoid garden-specific furniture, which at the time followed a pattern (either antique reproductions or rusticated pieces), looking instead for a quality and style equivalent to the furnishings indoors. The extensive publicity that later surrounded the garden prompted the furniture company's managing director, David Sutherland, to thank Luciano personally for his order and the boost it had given the company's profile.

The garden is both formal and relaxing, a withdrawing or receiving place with a quiet but confident air, framed by the delicate tracery of maple foliage, which creates flickering silhouettes after dark. It is theatrical in any light, looking out across the borrowed greenery of the gardens below. Although lighting plays a major part in the composition, it is subdued and subtle, washing the rendered walls or highlighting the deck from low down, to reduce glare.

Through this client Luciano was introduced to a network of clients and patrons, which enabled him to expand his remarkable portfolio of successful schemes. Meanwhile, the publicity surrounding the project launched his career into the international spotlight, encompassing *House & Garden* and several other influential magazines. At the client's insistence the garden was photographed from above, a viewpoint that revealed the ordered layout and showed the impact of the subtle lighting to good effect. Although a modest endeavour, the scheme set the tone for the future and the projects that would flow on a seemingly effortless creative tide. It brought Luciano from the theoretical world of his studies into the real world of garden design, with serious commissions and the development of a very particular style.

As Luciano's designs became more spatial than decorative, the book of photographs of Villa Gamberaia increasingly stimulated his thinking. Atmospheric and moody, the images haunted and mesmerized him. He wanted to seduce people into entering his gardens using the architecture of planting, the texture of surfaces and the arrangement of sculpture, containers and furniture. His intention was never to imitate but to explore, to understand the sentiment behind the garden and the intensely motivating images.

Luciano shares his response to the environment and our experience of it with a range of artists. Andy Goldsworthy senses the special qualities of local landscapes and places, connecting to and enhancing the spirit of a place using found objects or locally significant materials. Few other artists get so involved with the warp and weft of a landscape, or produce such emotive pieces. This interaction between art and land, its materials yielded up or scattered, collected or refashioned, is a fundamental part of Luciano's creative endeavour, and the grassed domes and ribbons of basalt on his roof garden in Geneva (pp. 57–69) are strongly influenced by Goldsworthy. Light is also crucial to Goldsworthy, who photographs his often short-lived work to reveal finely wrought curtains of twigs, ice forms or tapestries of leaf and petal, playing with the drama between light and shade to create mysterious beauty.

The artist James Turrell takes a simple concept, such as light, and works with colour to explore and reveal its true beauty and fascination. In many of his works he frames the sky, asking us to concentrate on these windows to infinity, which change with the movement of the sun, creating an atmospheric light show that evolves as time passes and puts the viewer in touch with

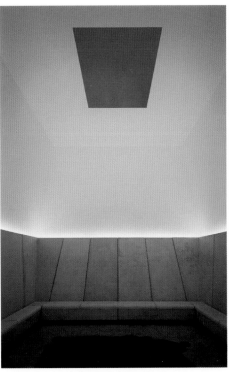

James Turrell focuses on mysterious and contemplative colour transitions in *Deer Shelter Skyspace* (2006) at the Yorkshire Sculpture Park.

Silent changes of light and mood, sublime and beguiling, are typical of his work.

Interior designer Christian Liaigre creates cool, understated rooms, keeping furniture lines low and allowing flowing space to dominate. An overwhelming sense of discreet luxury pervades his work.

a deeper sense of existence. Luciano finds himself returning to Turrell's *Deer Shelter Skyspace* in the Yorkshire Sculpture Park, near Wakefield, 'like a lover to an object of veneration'. Its tranquillity and reassurance fulfil a basic need that he rediscovers as he creates each new garden. Being able to change our response to our environment is what drives many designers, but Luciano's design specifically concerns light and shadow, surfaces and texture, depth and meaning. The silence of Turrell's work also resonates with Luciano and his gardens, where the act of appreciation needs no narrative.

Here the link with the formative Gamberaia images is most cogent. It is the detail of revealed texture, shadow and three-dimensional form that resonates within each composition, in a spiritual and elemental response. The mists and light-filled skies in many of the images help in the appreciation of scale and proportion, often the gift of black-and-white photographs over those in colour. The atmosphere captured in each image is the siren voice that Luciano finds impossible to resist, and what he feels he must re-create in his own work. A garden is not simply limestone, yew and lawn, but is greater than the sum of these elements, which are carefully chosen and manipulated to enhance its unique spirit. This emotionally charged view of garden design is shared by an elite within the profession. Luciano believes his craft and his approach are akin to those of the photographer, who must also convey the distinctive personality of each garden and landscape.

The interior designer Christian Liaigre has also greatly influenced Luciano, bridging the divide between art and design. Considered one of the most important contemporary designers, Liaigre creates pared-back rooms in which the careful arrangement of furniture, often at low level, allows the space itself to dominate. This architectural approach is echoed in Luciano's work. Liaigre's spaces have an almost external quality, while Luciano is inspired by Liaigre's interior art, using, in his

The architect John Pawson is famed for his expressive manipulation of light and shadow. His cool surface treatments and simple expanses of colour are typical of his minimalist work, with carefully hidden details creating an ethereal, floating quality. This is the staircase of his own house in London.

awnings, soft furnishings and paint finishes, colours and fabrics that are normally seen indoors. An attention to detail and craftsmanship equal to that shown in Liaigre's work is evident in Luciano's garden furniture, containers and paving, which are meticulously designed to allow space and light to flow seamlessly between building and garden. The two designers share an ability to create calm, comfortable and memorable spaces.

Japanese gardens and architecture provide meditative and sensual experiences with a similar message to Luciano's work. He mentions Tadao Ando, who in his strident and sculptural architecture plays with light and shadow on simple surfaces and forms. Although British, John Pawson expresses light, space and proportion in his strictly minimalist spaces in a very Japanese way. Luciano sees nature in the work of both men, and a connection to the meditative and ritualistic spaces of Zen gardens, with their simple palettes of materials that are so expressive and mesmerizing. His roof gardens in Geneva are testament to these influences, both in the materials used and in the careful placing of objects.

Luciano reveres the work of photographers Rolfe Horn and Michael Kenna. Although naturally he admires both composition and subject matter, it is the quality of the images and their atmosphere that speak to him particularly, and the way the camera interprets surfaces and materials. This graphic quality is linked closely in his gardens to the play of light and shadow, phenomena that he cannot change, but which he manipulates and exploits enthusiastically.

A fascination with light and its impact on surfaces, revealing glowing depth and detail, remains central to Luciano's work, his way of life and his thinking. All his schemes are informed and defined by light and shade, luminous surfaces and recessed shadow, sculptural forms and architecture revealed by sunlight in the daytime and atmospheric lighting at night. Such is the essence of Luciano Giubbilei.

The Design Process

Luciano relies on carefully crafted mood boards (previous pages) to communicate his ideas to clients. Initial sketches for the Geneva garden (right; pp. 57–69) and a finished perspective for the Laurent-Perrier garden at the RHS Chelsea Flower Show in 2009 (opposite; pp. 176–91) convey the spatial concepts.

Luciano describes his design approach as spatial art, in which the composition has a living quality, with elements that invite one to stay and drink in the experience. He regards each garden as a composition of forms placed to govern how one sees and experiences the whole. These sentiments were embodied in his design for the Laurent-Perrier garden at the Royal Horticultural Society's Chelsea Flower Show in 2009 (opposite, and pp. 176–91). Through the arrangement of elements he aimed to draw in the viewer, envisaging the garden as a sculpture to be experienced. More importantly, the comfort of the space was essential, and his intention was not to impress but to embrace, creating a spatial ambience of ease and familiarity.

Much of Luciano's work has come to him through interior designers who have set the tone of the space around which Luciano works and in which his clients live. He values this connection not only as a source of commissions but also because he respects the designers' ability to change spatial character. Many of the schemes in this book started with seating and social areas, which for him are fundamental reasons for creating a garden, and he sees parallels with that approach in interior design. The garden then works around this hub or relates to the architecture of the building. He is fascinated by the relationship between the creation of spaces within a box (the house or apartment) and those essentially outside that box. The positioning of objects and, more importantly, the voids between those objects are at the heart of his work, an approach that excites Luciano himself as much as the clients for whom he designs.

Luciano refers again and again to the graphic qualities of the Gamberaia book, and the photographs inspire the layering of his landscapes, both physically – in the organization of hedges of different species, a typical detail – and also intellectually, in his investigation of materials. Travertine is a favourite stone, and he has

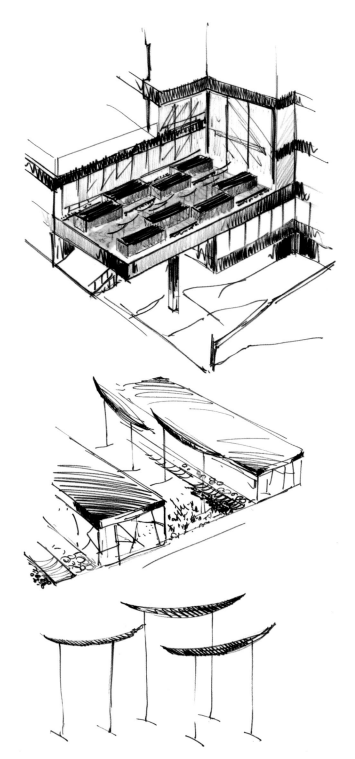

discovered many different ways of using it, each
providing subtle nuances in character and personality.

Luciano's depth of exploration and detail is missed
by many commentators, who see his work in purely
stylistic terms. For him each stone, each finish,
each hedge species and each specimen plant has
a resonance and meaning that he endeavours to
communicate to his clients, and the associations
of plants and constructed elements are carefully
considered. This comes across particularly in his
Morocco garden (pp. 114–33), where he embraced local
materials and products but channelled the skills of
the local craftsmen to produce a composition that is
immediately recognizable as his, while simultaneously
of a different place.

Luciano treats all ingredients within the garden
as equally important. Symmetry and repetition are

characteristic, and he meticulously develops dimensions
and spatial order in the design studio, a process
fundamental to the sharp, ordered schemes that result.
The clients must put their trust in this method, for
this sense of order and careful placement is essential
to Luciano's work, and the very reason why he would
have been commissioned.

The design process begins with a meeting with
the client, normally a general discussion during which
Luciano is careful not to lead the way by showing his
work. He wants his clients to reveal their intentions
honestly, without any bias. Only later will he show
and discuss his own body of work. He allows the
client to talk, guiding them and suggesting ideas only
in abstract. The discussion is a two-way interview,
in which client and designer are both looking for
compatibility and the ability to work together with

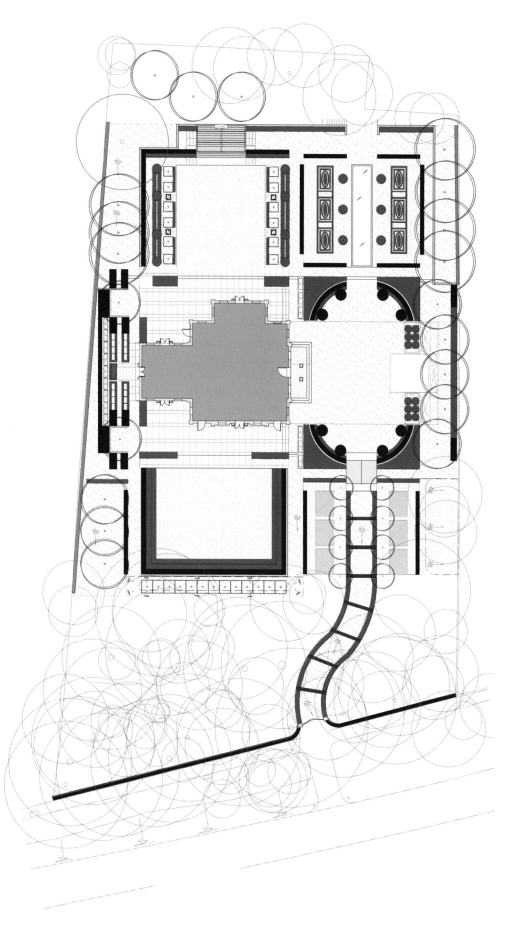

mutual respect. Luciano sets clear boundaries as to how the project is to progress and how design decisions will be made. He is fascinated by people – his clients especially – and pays attention to the way they combine furniture and fabrics, ornaments and paintings, colours and textures. He is intrigued by both the love and attention given to the minutiae of objects placed with care and the decision to create the upheaval of a new garden.

Once engaged, Luciano visits and carefully analyses the site and its character, and commissions a detailed survey as a basis for design development. Often he experiences an immediate reaction, returning to the office with his mind ticking over with ideas. He carries a small sketchbook in which he records the instant responses that underpin his creativity. The pages show notes, sketched ideas and layouts that often form part of the final solution in some way.

These basic notions evolve into loose layouts, but always Luciano's thinking coalesces around images. Mood boards (see pp. 20–21) are produced with atmospheric photographs, materials and surfaces, sometimes supported by samples. The intention is to concentrate the client's mind on the experience of the garden and their response to it, and Luciano presents a range of design options and images to encourage discussion. The information is accompanied by a simple pencil sketch of the site layout, which is later converted into a three-dimensional computer-generated model supported by a selection of views. At this stage there are no scale drawings and little fine detail; the presentation is made verbally in order to elicit a response.

By contrast with this fluid opening to Luciano's schemes, the designs are finally embodied in what his office staff call 'beige plans', precise computer-generated drawings of the layouts, which belie the sketchiness of the early ideas. For larger schemes he

Accurate computer-generated plans and sections are supported by a three-dimensional computer model, which enables the client to understand and even 'walk' the proposed garden. This one was for a private client in Hertfordshire.

asks interior designer and graphic artist Alan Hughes, with whom he has worked since 1999, to produce three-dimensional views. These drawings have a softness and inherent beauty that only hand-rendering can produce, and lend personality to the somewhat cooler recordings of the beige plans, using colour and a range of viewpoints to inject the necessary lifeblood into the projects. They also reveal the strength of the forms used to build the garden.

A mood board also accompanies the second presentation, and, as materials are finalized, Luciano introduces specifics, finally preparing the scheme for the process of tendering for and choosing a suitable contractor. At this point samples and images of actual or close copies of materials and artefacts are revealed. He often asks specialist craftsmen to prepare sample details of such structures as pergolas for the approval of the client, and material samples are used as much as possible in order to paint a clear and meaningful picture of the intended scheme. Through forging a close working relationship with craftsmen Luciano is able to identify very precisely how such elements will look within a new scheme. The inclusion of artists' work is very different, however, and there the client often leads, allowing greater consensus. These fascinating discussions often include the artists themselves.

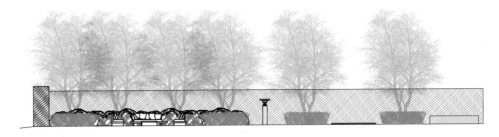

Luciano enjoys the process of reflection on the work he produces. Discussions with clients, his design staff, journalists and other designers help him to fine-tune his work, ensuring that the finished gardens are exactly as he intends. His ability to think clearly in three dimensions means that when the garden is complete he will be happy, knowing that he has seen it before, carefully pieced together like a jigsaw. His confidence has grown considerably since he graduated, although he still likes to spend as much time at the site as possible. An important time for reflection, and one that he is careful to allow himself, is just before

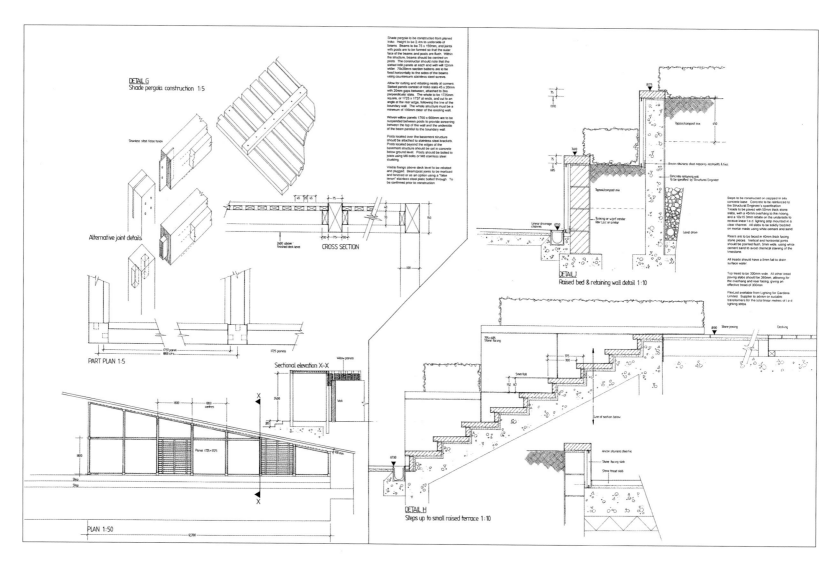

DETAIL G
Shade pergola construction 1:5

Stainless steel false tenon

Alternative joint details

CROSS SECTION

PART PLAN 1:5

Sectional elevation X-X

PLAN 1:50

DETAIL J
Raised bed & retaining wall detail 1:10

DETAIL H
Steps up to small raised terrace 1:10

As the design process becomes more detailed, working drawings are produced. Above, a series of details explains the construction of such elements as steps and walls to the contractor building the Boltons garden (pp. 29–41). A second drawing (right) shows the specific decorative elements to be used in the garden.

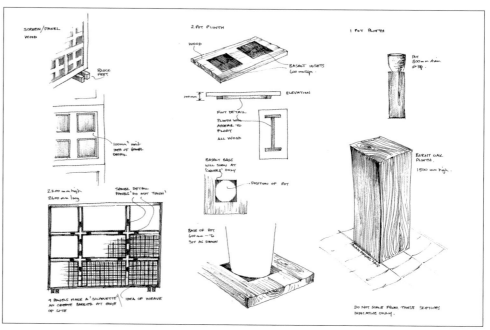

For the first phase of the
Geneva garden (pp. 57–69),
Swiss architect Daniel
Grataloup (below, left)
produced three-dimensional
maquettes to create and
communicate the scale
and surface of the
hemispherical forms.

contracts are signed and construction starts. There
is always room for improvement, and he feels more
comfortable once he has processed the design ideas
in this way.

Luciano prefers to work with a known and trusted
contractor (often Landform Consultants, with which
he has built many gardens) that will deliver the level
of quality he requires, but as his overseas commissions
increase he ensures that as much detail as possible is
present in the drawings and specifications. This is the
best way of controlling the standard of his work, and
he uses a universal visual language whenever he can.
He also visits regularly during construction, eager
to be part of the fine-tuning and decision-making,
and – perhaps more importantly – to see his cherished
creations taking shape. Direct communication is
an essential part of his service, and ensures that
his contractors and specialists feel supported.

Having achieved a high level of quality and poise
in his work, Luciano is not resting on his laurels.
He relished his first experience of the Chelsea Flower
Show in London in 2009, and is already planning
his next garden there, but he is also ready for more
challenges and looking for ways in which he can refine
and develop his abilities. During the creation of his
spectacular Laurent-Perrier garden he reflected on
his design process and the way in which his studio
works. The use of perennials and grass mixes – seen
for the first time in that garden – has changed his
whole attitude to colour and plant associations, and
the asymmetry of Japanese and Modernist design
also appeals tremendously. This all presents new
opportunities for his work, and he is determined to
expand his horizons, hoping to take his clients with
him. For now, he reveals the story so far through a
carefully selected range of his gardens.

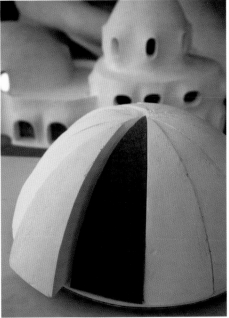

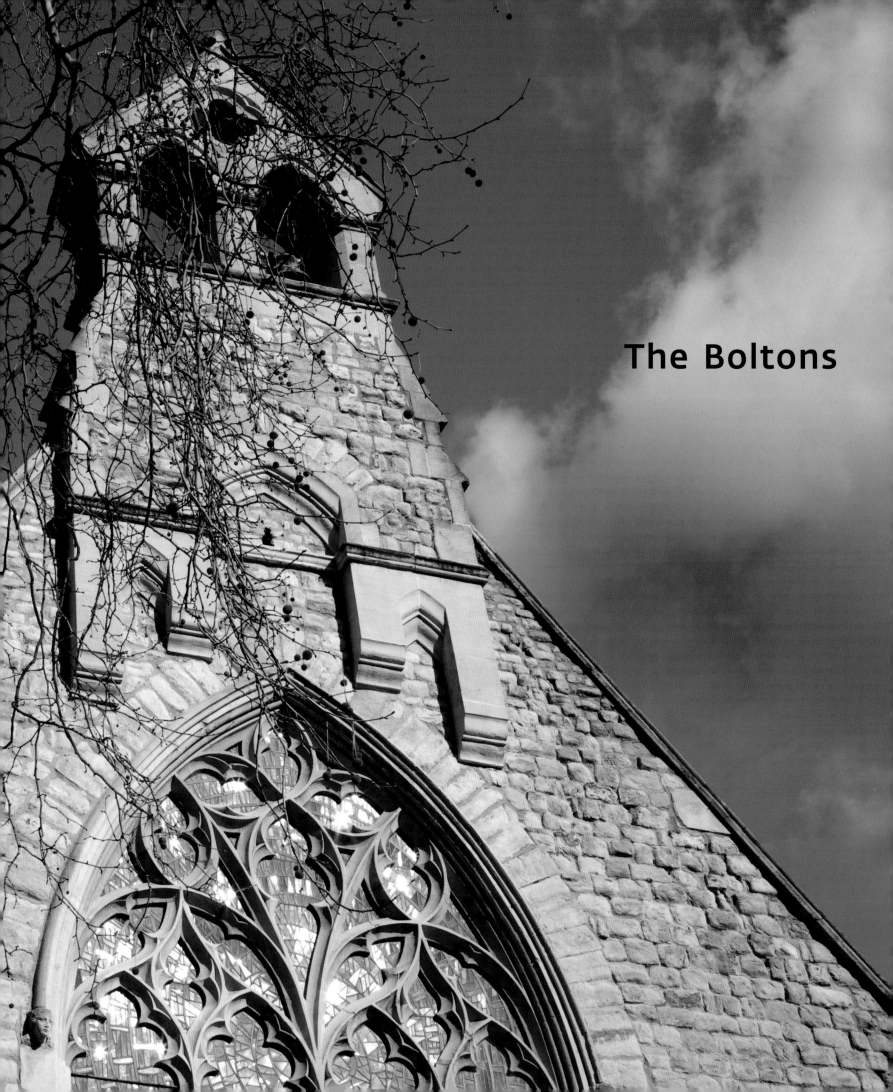

The Boltons

THE BOLTONS

LONDON
2001

PRINCIPAL USE
Private residence

DESIGN
1999–2000

CONSTRUCTION
2000–2001

GARDEN AREA
1500 sq. m (16,100 sq. ft)

This project was Luciano's first collaboration with interior designer Kelly Hoppen, who admired his attention to detail and the high level of quality he achieved. Since the house was simultaneously being extended into the garden, Luciano also worked with the client's architect, and was fascinated by the opportunity to integrate architecture, interior and garden.

The set-up was not without its problems, however: the architect wanted Luciano to use its contractor, but by now he had built up a special relationship with Mark Gregory of Landform Consultants, who had produced several successful schemes for him. After some discussion the project went ahead with Landform as contractor, and with a clear line between the responsibilities for garden and house.

The trapezoidal plot is widest by the house. Luciano began by placing various interior services and utilities, which had to be located in the garden, within a screened compound, leaving an L-shaped space. A regular layout was then carved out of the angled site, pulling away from the awkward boundaries and transforming the scale, proportion and perception of the composition. The existing walls were softened and unified with woven willow hurdles.

A generous terrace flows from the house, providing space for relaxation and outdoor dining. A raised-ground-floor terrace is paved in iroko deck boards picked up in the etched pattern on the glass of the roof lights. Both areas accommodate the Sutherland furniture that Luciano first used in Harcourt Terrace (see pp. 14–16).

For the paving and wall cladding, Luciano was obliged to work with the Portland stone specified by the architect. This high-quality limestone is rich in fossils and sedimentary pattern, and a pale cream colour when first quarried. It is a characteristic stone in London, defining many of the city's landmarks, but its porosity means that through a chemical reaction with rainwater it gradually becomes a whitish grey. (Luciano has managed to remedy this in later schemes by using different finishes.) The paving is laid in stack bond, with a strong grid of joints, and the rectangular slabs running perpendicular to the house produce a sense of movement into the garden.

An elegant, full-width flight of steps leads up to the main lawn, giving the garden a generous proportion. From here the design is predominantly soft, focusing on the architecture of the planting. This was the first of Luciano's commissions where the budget allowed the use of mature specimens, providing the garden with a clear structure and creating immediate impact. Luciano ordered specific plants from specialist growers in Belgium and The Netherlands, but also saw the nurseries as sources of inspiration, fleshing out his ideas as he meandered through the stock fields.

Lines of yew cubes (*Taxus baccata*) run the length of the garden, creating solids and voids that create sharply defined shadows and pools of light. A limestone-gravel path runs alongside, providing a structured walk that allows changing glimpses of the garden through the narrow gaps between specimens. Framing the large lawn closest to the house are long, low cushions of box (*Buxus sempervirens*) in two different heights. Pleached hornbeam (*Carpinus betulus*) floats above the box for privacy and strong vertical structure, and greater screening is provided by tall cubes of lime (*Tilia* x *europaea* 'Pallida'), which disguise the boundaries and were slotted in among several existing trees. Beds under the lime trees are flooded with autumn-flowering Japanese anemone (*Anemone* x *hybrida* 'Honorine Jobert'). For most of the season this plant provides textured greenery, but as autumn approaches its pure-white flowers dance in the air, ethereal beyond the arcades of yew.

Lighting is used chiefly at low level to wash the lawn, pathway and paving, emphasizing the planting structure and picking out the trunks and base of the canopy of the pleached hornbeams. Besides urns on slender plinths, acting as focal points, there is little additional decoration or art in the garden: it is the architecture of the planting and the changing quality of light that are enshrined in this project and produce the sense of space.

Luciano also designed the front garden, continuing his use of Portland paving and limestone gravel, into which he positioned cubes of box hedging. This pared-back approach prepares the eye for the major composition in the back garden.

It was not until May 2001, when the project was completed, that the clients met Luciano and saw the garden at first hand. Since they had been living overseas and Hoppen had effectively taken on their role, Luciano had not realized that they had been enthusiastically following the scheme through her. On first seeing the garden – a magical moment for Luciano – they were overwhelmed by its beauty and presence. The love affair continues, and, as a precious part of the client's home environment, the garden is still maintained by Landform.

Luciano describes the upheaval involved in the creation of a new garden as a disturbance out of which the garden gradually emerges into a state of peace and tranquillity, when silence descends to reveal that a scheme has reached completion. He felt this transition most profoundly in this project, and sees it as a timeless composition that resonates with a spiritual quality, a description that is fully endorsed by his client.

I see the creation of the garden as a journey, moving gradually to achieve a sense of silence.

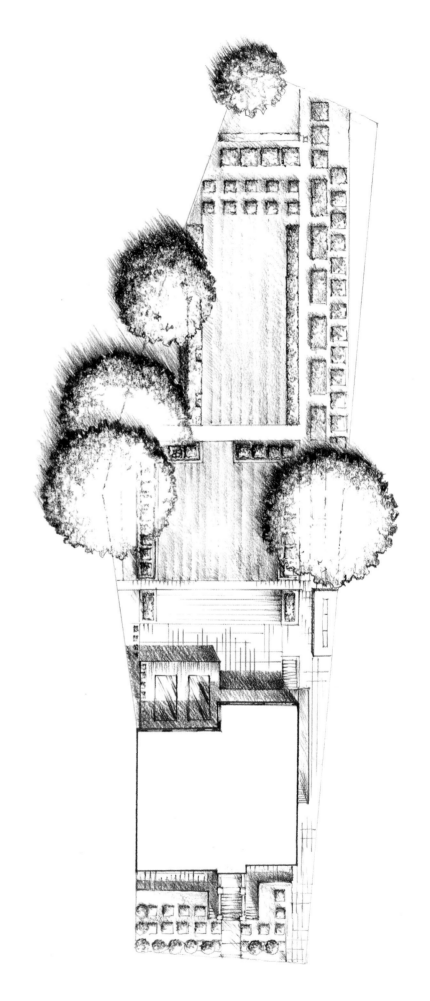

LEFT A simple architectural composition of gravel, clipped box cubes and pleached *Tilia* x *europaea* 'Pallida' creates stylish privacy in the front garden.

OPPOSITE An overview shows the importance of the wide limestone steps rising into the main space.

OPPOSITE, LEFT, AND RIGHT
The lower-level terrace is
the main entertaining space.

OPPOSITE, TOP RIGHT Willow
hurdles are a favourite
screen for Luciano, a
textured backdrop for
sculpture and ornament.

OPPOSITE, BOTTOM RIGHT
The ipe deck of the first-
floor terrace is patterned
by the shadow of the
balustrade.

Pelham Crescent

PELHAM CRESCENT

LONDON
2004

PRINCIPAL USE
Private residence

DESIGN
2003

CONSTRUCTION
2003–2004

GARDEN AREA
140 sq. m (1500 sq. ft)

The quiet serenity of this design is quite different from that of Luciano's other gardens. That may owe something to its more intimate scale and the emphasis on trees and reflecting surfaces rather than on the architecture of hedges and expanses of lawn.

As happens with many older London properties, a new family brought new needs, and the client had engaged an architect to redevelop and open up this Grade I-listed building. Simultaneously they realized that the garden would also need to be developed. They had noticed Luciano's work on the Boltons in *Architectural Digest*, and were introduced to him by their interior designer, Gilly Holloway.

The site appealed to Luciano, who immediately felt the need for a strong relationship between house and garden in terms of scale and proportion. The far end of the plot had been redeveloped to incorporate a new garage, which also provided access to the main garden. As a result Luciano was required to develop a space between the house and a new pavilion for relaxation and family entertainment immediately in front of the garage. One enters the garden either from below at basement level or from above at street level, a typical arrangement for London houses and one that plays with perspective.

The pavilion provides both a focus for the garden when seen from the house and a place from which to look back at the house. The tall property shelters the garden from the noise of the city but also, with its elongated facade, emphasizes the narrowness of the space.

Although hedges are used in the garden, box (*Buxus sempervirens*) and hornbeam (*Carpinus betulus*) screen and soften the boundary walls rather than creating enclosures or spatial structure. As the seasons change, the evergreen box remains constant but the hornbeam's old foliage, held on the tree, turns a pale copper colour in harmony with the garden's timber detailing. In a departure from his previous emphasis on formal green architecture, Luciano introduced a line of multi-stemmed *Amelanchier* running the length of the garden and creating a light, elegant canopy structure. The dark branches contrast strongly with the gravel below, creating strong silhouettes and tracery patterns. The soft, rounded foliage provides vibrant autumn colour, and in spring the canopies are dense with ivory blossom, allowing the garden to change its character with the seasons.

The hard-materials palette is restrained and limited to a soft-honed Acero limestone for the water feature, complemented by limestone gravel and Scala blue flame-textured limestone for the steps and paving.

This creates a neutral yet sophisticated surface that sets off the planting and allows the architecture of house and pavilion to be appreciated.

The water feature provided Luciano with his first opportunity to work with Andrew Ewing, a London-based water specialist producing bespoke sculptural forms with water as their focus. The long plinth that resulted from their collaboration not only connects the two ends of the garden, but also, more importantly, with its reflective surface allows a play of dappled and changing light that interacts with the tree canopies above.

Jets gently ripple water across the surface, constantly refreshing and cleaning the stone and revealing the delicate fossil content and colour within it. A narrow slot allows the water to drain invisibly and silently into the reservoir beneath. Occasionally leaves drop on to the surface, and on one of his subsequent visits, Luciano was delighted to find the children playing with the water, engrossed and captivated by its magical qualities. Birds are also frequent visitors, skimming the surface and bathing in the shallow film of shimmering liquid. This sense of abundance in the water flow – quiet and constant, like a natural spring – was something for which Luciano had been searching.

Small plinths were inserted into the hedging to accommodate three black-oak sculptures by Malcolm Martin and Gaynor Dowling, mirroring the position of the three trees. The pieces stand like sentinels, all the same height although subtly different. The oak is charred for protection, creating an intense blackness that echoes the writhing ebony stems of the *Amelanchier*. From the house the sculptures are hidden in their recesses, and they reveal themselves only as the journey through the garden begins, repeating the underlying rhythm of the space.

While the garden has an undeniable beauty by day, it is at night that it comes alive. The pavilion provides a clear destination and a source of light that draws one through the garden, creating an opposing force to balance the elevation of the house. Theatrical lighting is achieved with very few fittings, washing the walls or glowing behind planters to create carefully placed pools of light with corresponding shadows.

Each tree is lit from below so that the light catches the canopy edges or the tracery of the bare branches, according to the season. Fibre-optic lighting placed beneath the water jets creates a candle-like effect, giving a mysterious sparkle to the reflective monolith. The low positioning of the various fittings produces an ethereal quality, transforming the space and inverting the usual lighting direction. The garden dissolves into the shadows, playful but mysterious.

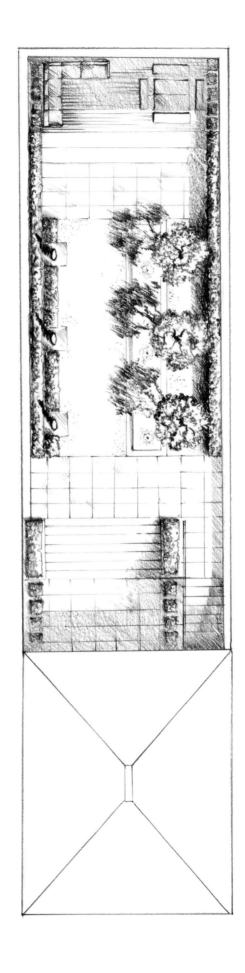

I consciously moved away from formal structure and wanted to allow the space itself to speak; it did, both to me and to my clients.

BELOW AND OPPOSITE, TOP AND BOTTOM RIGHT The changing moods of the multi-stemmed *Amelanchier* trees through the seasons provide a structural focus, ideal in a narrow urban plot.

OPPOSITE, BOTTOM LEFT The fabric-like finish of the chiselled charred-oak sculptures by Martin and Dowling create eye-catching relief within the hornbeam hedges.

Andrew Ewing's low, rectangular water feature is a resonant centrepiece. Fibre-optic lighting creates a flickering, candle-like impression of water and light, connecting house and garden as a single composition.

Geneva

GENEVA
SWITZERLAND
2002/2009

PRINCIPAL USE
Part of corporate headquarters

DESIGN
2001–2002; 2008–2009

CONSTRUCTION
2001–2002; 2008–2009

GARDEN AREA
1700 sq. m/18,000 sq. ft
(Phase 1); 2570 sq. m/
27,600 sq. ft (Phase 2)

For the most part Luciano designs private gardens, but he made an exception for a Swiss private investment company, Unigestion, intrigued by its owner and his love of art, which he generously introduces into the workplace for the enjoyment of his employees. Having completed a tiny commission for the same client in London, Luciano was invited to the company's headquarters (which was being transformed by architectural practice Ris Chabloz) and commissioned to design two roof spaces.

The brief for Phase 1 – the higher of the two levels, immediately outside the staff canteen and relaxation area – was for a three-dimensional installation that would convey a sense of profound tranquillity and calm while motivating the team. Luciano's scheme was inspired by land art fused with a Japanese philosophy of abstraction from the landscape, the innate spirit of objects and the spatial relationships between them. Invisible from the street, it inspires curiosity once one emerges from the lift.

The design's minimalist character suits the Modernist tone of the Unigestion building, but is also seen against the backdrop of Geneva's older buildings. While the client and Unigestion's employees were enthusiastic about the scheme, Luciano had by law to consult the residents of the surrounding apartments who shared a view of the roof garden; to his relief, they too were supportive of and fascinated by the design.

The most notable element of the design is a series of nine domes that appear to emerge from the structure of the building, diminishing in size as they curve across the space from the largest, 4.2 metres in diameter and 2.2 metres high (14 x 7 ft). The garden was to be built by the family company of a fellow student from Inchbald, Aude Jacquet, who introduced Luciano to the architect Daniel Grataloup, who took up the cause of the domes. Grataloup created lightweight versions in polystyrene and fibreglass, entrancing Luciano with his eccentric studio and his insistence on working by hand rather than relying on computers. By means of models, collages and drawings they produced the geometric forms.

Since weight and maintenance were an important consideration, the domes could not be planted. One of the engineers suggested that they be covered in synthetic grass, tailored to their curved forms. Initially Luciano was horrified at such artificiality, but, after seeing the samples, he started to feel that the solution answered all aspects of the brief. He was finally persuaded by the client, who felt strongly that the visual effect was most important.

Luciano flooded the roof surface with tumbled Carrara marble chippings, creating a glowing white backdrop for the domes. In direct contrast, parallel lines of split, open-face Belgian basalt race across the gravel in broken sequences, perpendicular to the building, creating movement and rhythm with dark shadows. Here Luciano draws a direct link to the Japanese idea that nature is reflected in stones and rocks as much as plants. In typical Zen style the whole composition is bordered by a dark strip of pebbles – in this case Italian black granite – contained by fine metal edging.

The tranquil playfulness of this first phase has proved popular with staff, who see it as an extension of the artworks in the building. The play of soft light and shadow on the domes certainly provides a fascinating and distracting backdrop to their daily routines, and Luciano's client sends him images of the garden in different seasons, obviously thrilled with the installation.

Phase 2 was completed in 2009 on the first floor, one level below the domes. Only overlooking properties can see the two phases together; from inside the offices there is no visual relationship. Luciano wanted to use a similar approach and palette of materials as for Phase 1, with subtle differences. The space is more linear and restricted, and that is reflected in the raised stone boxes and strips of stone and black pebbles that run parallel to the building.

The low boxes are lightweight steel frames 2.5 x 1 metre (8 x 3 ft), clad in split-face slate of varying depths to look like strata. They are topped with shallow copings of Ardesia smooth black stone, laid as single pieces to create surreal reflective surfaces that add to the stillness of the space while simultaneously suggesting rhythm and movement. Straddling the lines of pebbles and strips of stone, the boxes hold the composition together and fix the elegant geometry.

Between the linear borders, large rectangles of ground-hugging sedum create carpets of foliage texture that break up the simple gravel surface. In narrower sections of the terrace the sedum stretches out more expansively and the pattern of the boxes becomes less ordered. Here the surrounding tree canopies enclose the space in typical Japanese fashion, where borrowed scenery forms part of the composition. The Japanese references are unmistakable, with the simple fenestration and roof overhang on one side and the dark bordered gravel on the other: a Western–Zen fusion.

From above, both gardens have a strongly graphic quality, emphasized by the simple palette of contrasting materials. From inside the building, the glowing spaces suggest subtle movement and mesmerizing tranquillity, and form inspiring backdrops for both staff and neighbours to share.

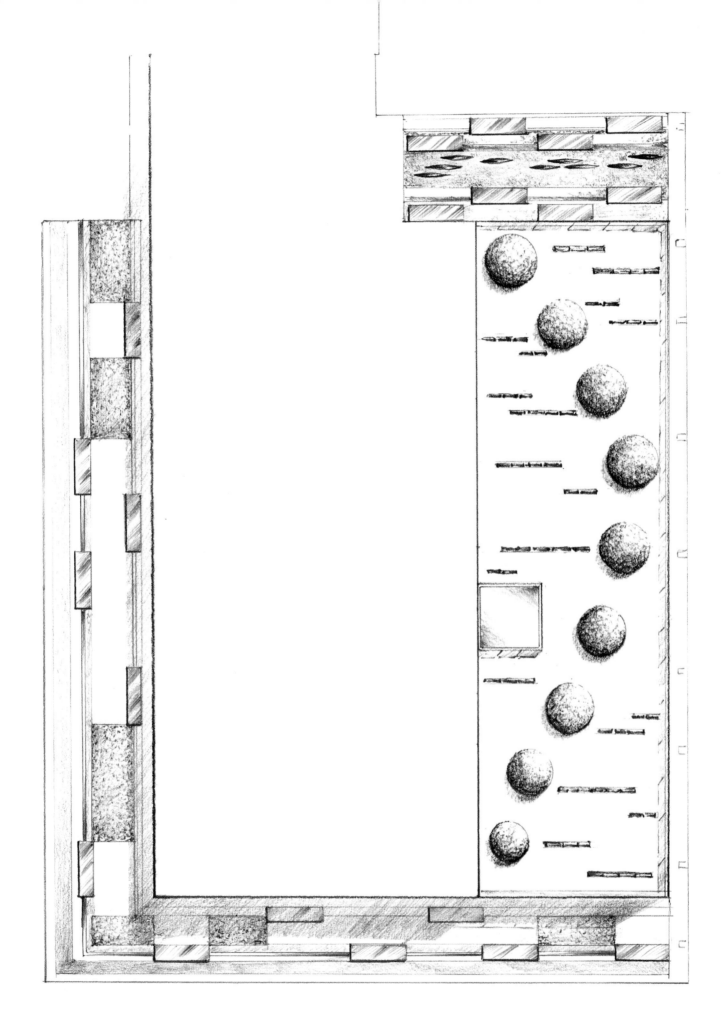

The plinths, a key element of the Phase 2 garden, are of black Ardesia stone over riven silver slate side walls. Rectangular blocks of sedum provide low carpets of foliage texture and colour emerging through the luminous gravel.

FAR LEFT The dark pebbles (top) that border the Phase 1 garden provide a link with the detailing of the second phase (bottom).

LEFT, OPPOSITE AND OVERLEAF The synthetic-grass domes of Phase 1 dominate the scheme, their soft forms revealed by light in contrast with the sea of pale gravel and the ribs of dark basalt that stretch across the roof.

I wanted to create spaces that took people out of themselves: playful but spiritual.

Wentworth

WENTWORTH

SURREY, ENGLAND
2009

PRINCIPAL USE
Private residence

DESIGN
2007

CONSTRUCTION
2008–2009

GARDEN AREA (REAR)
3300 sq. m (35,500 sq. ft)

The invitation to design for a client who had recently purchased a villa on the exclusive Wentworth estate, to the west of London, came in 2007. The family was relocating from a smaller property elsewhere on the estate, and the new house was undergoing extensive refurbishment. Mature woodland surrounds the property, creating the sense of a garden within a landscape, quite different from the contained spaces with which Luciano works in London. Similarly, the house has a certain grandeur: it is wide and massive, like a liner in the landscape. Most importantly, the garden contained changes of level, which Luciano instinctively knew he needed to use. A densely planted terrace with a complex layout stood close to the house, blocking views into the garden, and a swimming pool (which was to be retained) stood alongside. The site needed to be more coherent.

Luciano saw the terrace as the main device with which to connect house and garden, and his first step was to expand it. Following the proportions of the house a formal layout took shape with mainly paved surfaces, a plan that the owners questioned at first. Such seismic changes can be unnerving for a client, but Luciano was resolute, confident that the spacious interiors and grand facade needed a gesture that could compete and sit happily alongside. After the initial presentation the clients were firmly in agreement, and the garden subsequently changed little.

The terrace floats out into the garden at the same level as the house, and is wide enough to accommodate a dining area, lounging space, a shaded pergola and an outdoor fireplace. The paved areas are dominant and generous, separated by a central rectangle of lawn but defined by low lines of box hedging (*Buxus sempervirens*) and dome specimens with narrow garlands of table-pruned plane trees (*Platanus* x *hispanica*) that seem to float above. Their slender trunks are echoed in the simple architecture of the timber pergola, which has been left to silver with age, giving a sense of lightness to the space. The terrace is often bathed in sunlight, and the shadow patterns running across the surfaces produce a transitory architecture of their own.

For Luciano, the sequence of spaces relies almost entirely on scale and proportion. The pale expanses of gridded limestone slabs and the slender elegance of the fragile table-pruned trees are part of the same narrative, a slowing down of the pace between the house and the softer, greener garden beyond.

Near by, the swimming pool was given a facelift with new tiling and terrace paving with deck inserts. This made it an integral part of the scheme, and allowed the strict grid of paving to run across the whole space. When left unlit after dark, its surface is reflective. Existing trees and new planting were lit with some subtlety, creating ghostly images on the surface of the water. The concept behind the lighting is one of mood and comfort, avoiding glare at all costs; it is restricted to uplighting and low-level horizontal washes. The use and manipulation of lighting has become a trademark of Luciano's design work, and forms an essential part of its contemporary ethos.

Although there was already a change of level in the garden, the higher area (by the house) was extended outwards to give the new terrace a more pleasing proportion. For the main garden below, Luciano wanted a sense of contrast. Beyond a narrow line of gravel, which sweeps round the main lawn in a huge apse, the formality of the garden gives way to a wilder, looser quality, softened by retained trees, which add height and maturity. A crisp, narrow hedge of box defines the boundary between old and new, punctuated by beehive topiary yews (*Taxus baccata*).

The central steps down to the lawn appear to float, especially in the evening, when the under-step LEDs are at work. As it leads from one level to the next, the pale limestone flight slices through the dark, textured hedging on either side, which masks the retaining wall. The gravel strip that defines the lawn runs out into the garden, round an existing tree, and back again, creating an incidental focus as one enters the lower area. This coming together of the formal and the accidental appeals to Luciano in all his work, creating nuances that mark out each scheme as individual.

The second phase of the scheme concentrated on the arrival court at the front of the house, and retained many of the basic principles of the overall design by way of an introduction. Pale resin-bonded gravel is used for the driveway with simple blocks of limestone paving to provide consistency with the main terrace to the rear. The existing mature trees were all retained, and simple cushions and domes of box structure the space and guide the eye.

The scheme bears the obvious signature of Luciano, but the client's comfort and functional and aesthetic needs are evident in the result, a garden that is inseparable from the family and from the spaces in which they live.

*Proportion, dimension and rhythm
run through my work:
key qualities that define the
spaces and the detailing.*

The light, open pergola links the fireplace to the terrace, but also frames views out across the sequence of ordered spaces. Dynamic shadow patterns play on the smooth, pale surfaces.

The subtlety of the lighting throughout the garden suits the calm grandeur of the space. Light floods out here from inside the house to create fan patterns of light across the paving. Floor-mounted uplighters and hidden step lights create a soft and muted glow to surfaces and planting on the terrace (overleaf); the pool is left unlit.

The Artists

NIGEL HALL

BORN
1943

WORKS
London

For Nigel Hall the landscape is a source of wonder. He regularly treks through the mountains of Switzerland, revelling in the space, especially when snow renders the terrain purer and more graphic. Deserts and oceans are other haunting favourites, apparently simple and silent but brooding with energy and power. Much of this dynamic is embodied in his work. In his studio he explores ideas through what he calls 'messy drawings', all thumbprints and atmospheric charcoal, but true beauty emerges in his sculptures, which are generally fashioned from wood.

In his works intended for gardens Hall uses bronze or Cor-ten steel, since they last longer, although the results are the same in terms of form. He works on the basis of previous ideas, and so his sculptures and drawings form a continuous evolution, each idea borrowing from or building on a previous notion or exploration. An evident recurring theme is that of two elements that exist together, creating symmetry and unity but never given equal weight.

A strong Japanese influence in Hall's work has developed through direct observation. Japan's quiet Zen gardens thrill and fascinate him, although he is always surprised by their small size. Their deft sense of scale is evident, however, and Hall recalls noticing

Hall produces preparatory drawings before moving into three dimensions by making timber maquettes (see also previous pages). The three-dimensional rhythms and qualities can then be better understood.

how they use borrowed landscape to expand and influence the mind. Mountains, trees and plants in the space beyond are all used as part of the composition.

Essential to Hall's sculptures is this sense of being part of the landscape and interacting with it. Although he has not produced many pieces specifically for a garden setting, he feels it is an appropriate environment for his work, being quieter and more controlled. His works are more commonly placed in wider landscape settings, although – curiously – much of his early work was influenced by landscape but intended for indoor installation. His work has gradually moved outdoors and become more clearly linked with its settings.

Hall confesses to 'becoming engrossed' in his work, fantasizing occasionally about a potential location. Few of his pieces are site-specific, but he does enjoy this detailed sense of synergy. One of his most celebrated sculptures, *Soglio* (1994), was located for several years at the Cass Sculpture Foundation, a large outdoor sculpture gallery on the Goodwood estate, West Sussex, established by Wilfred and Jeannette Cass in collaboration with the Arts Council. A massive Cor-ten circle with a slicing vertical bar, the piece was placed at the end of a long ride through

Hall's large studio allows sizeable pieces to be developed in controlled conditions, and provides a good interaction with light and shadow, which are fundamental to Nigel's work. The piece shown opposite is *Shared Sky 11* (1986), bronze.

the woodland, but in a slight depression and close to the long flint wall that surrounds the site. Hall's intention was to play with scale, so that the true size of the work was realized only as one came close.

Hall feels his methods are in tune with Luciano's not simply because of the clear sense of order and structure in the latter's gardens but also because of his attention to detail and careful planning. That is also how Hall likes to work, creating a sense of purity and strength through careful, precise planning and specification, and perfecting his forms by making models and maquettes. Light and shadow play an important part in his compositions, integrating and changing the impression as one moves around the installations. For Hall that is the key to sculpture as a medium: that it becomes a whole experience as the work blends with its context – much more dynamic than painting.

Hall has been involved with and present at the siting of all his sculptures, and sees this as an essential part of the process. He is always armed with a compass, which enables him to consider carefully how the light will move across the work and how the resulting shadows will interact. This was particularly striking with the wall-mounted sculpture *Big Bite* in Luciano's

Laurent-Perrier garden at the RHS Chelsea Flower Show in 2009 (see pp. 176–91). The interconnecting circles produced shadows that slowly and silently traversed the travertine and were reflected in the pool below. Hall admits that he was cautious about including his sculpture in the Chelsea show, and that he agreed only because he would be working with Luciano, confident that the results would be satisfactory.

Hall's first collaboration with Luciano had come with the Addison Crescent commission (see pp. 99–113). *Double Ellipse*, a piece in phosphor bronze (an alloy of bronze, copper and tin), sits high on the rendered wall and effectively ties the garden together as a single composition. The curved forms seem to float above the garden yet form a link with the rhythms of the tiered hedges. For Hall, this combination of stillness and rhythm – seen as one moves around and interacts with the sculpture – is meditative, a concept that he feels is present in all his work, the result of a process of simplification and refining. It is a principle that Luciano would echo with enthusiasm.

STEPHEN COX

BORN
1946

WORKS
Shropshire

There must always be a connection between the artist, the place and the human response, and Stephen Cox seems to manage this with ease. Luciano first came across his work when studying at Inchbald, on one of the most important site visits of the diploma programme: to the Cass Sculpture Foundation at Goodwood, West Sussex, a dramatic and sculptural place in its own right.

Two sculptures by Cox were in the Foundation's collection at that time: *Granite Catamarans on a Granite Wave* (1994), an eerie piece giving the sensation of standing underwater, almost as if drowning; and *Organs of Action* (1987–88) a group of forms nestled in a shallow grassy depression, a sculpture that Luciano was to see again in the garden in Kensington (see pp. 151–61).

Cox is fascinated by history and the traditions that permeate human society. Born in Bristol and trained at the Central School of Art and Design (Central Saint Martins College of Art and Design) in London, he has since both travelled and lived further afield. Italy, Egypt and India remain close to his heart, and their influences are woven into the work he produces. In India he sees ancient techniques that part the waves of centuries and make contact between sculptural artwork and the natural stone from which it emerges; in Egypt he sees

a culture in which such traditions have been lost, and which would benefit from their reintroduction; and in Italy he observes impressive machine-driven manufacturing and strong links between quarry and factory. Driven to explore the production of contemporary objects by means of ancient techniques, and the way in which the two opposing forces interact, he maintains strong connections with these countries as well as having a base in the UK, developing his theories and applying them to his sculpture, which he exhibits widely. Ultimately he sees his work as allied with the European tradition of mark-making, often incising the surfaces of his sculptures or building up surface texture, playing with light, shade and pattern.

Many of Cox's sculptures are created as individual, singular pieces, but occasionally he is commissioned to produce site-specific work, such as his monolithic sculpture for the University of Kent, *Hymn* (1991), which stands on a low rise and connects visually with Canterbury Cathedral in the distance. One of his *Catamaran* sculptures is now installed on a quayside in Jersey, forming the connection with the sea for which he had always hoped.

In gardens Cox is happy to make the connection between sculpture and spatial design, sometimes

Cox's studio is an Aladdin's cave of maquettes and trial pieces, which litter the surfaces as he explores textures and finishes. The view from the studio to the garden creates constant contact with nature and changing light. Seen here are: (right, from left) *Golden Ladder Heads, Up* (2001); maquettes of the Madonna and St Mildred for Lincoln College, Oxford; *Nepal Throng* (2002), black Indian granite; drawings for a project; and (opposite, left and top right) details of *Nepal Throng*.

choosing intimate pieces and sometimes introducing huge, dominant works. He will create anything from a hand-held bowl to a 15-tonne monolith that must be craned into place. Scale is the key consideration, but otherwise, he says, there must be 'nothing formulaic – the piece has to feel right'. He prefers to assist with the positioning of the work when possible, discussing it with the designer and the client, although on the several occasions when he has not been involved he has been amazed at the thoughtfulness and beauty of the final effect. A Hampshire garden originally designed by Sir Edwin Lutyens – which now contains one of Cox's pieces – represented one such occasion, and remains in his mind as the perfect composition of art and garden combined.

Cox remembers the installation of the sculptures in Luciano's Kensington garden (pp. 151–61) and the detailed discussions that led to the siting of the work. Originally the pieces were to be arranged in a wide circle, looking inwards, almost conversational. However, the scale and layout of the garden and house rendered this impossible, and eventually the individual elements were aligned to face the wide picture window. The conversational nature of the first arrangement was preserved, beckoning people into the intimate garden.

This sense of discovery and connection appeals to Cox. Sometimes when clients move house his commissions are left behind to take on a new life with the next family or owner. At Waddesdon Manor in Buckinghamshire Cox was commissioned by Lord Rothschild to create a sculpture for a recently discovered 'lost' garden. As its artefacts and treasures were yielded up, Cox envisaged his work perhaps being rediscovered and treasured or appreciated anew in the years to come.

Cox sees great beauty and poise in Luciano's work, and a minimalism in which the mind is concentrated on the precision and order of the composition. Sculpture is an intrinsic part of this story, not an addition or an extra that can be moved or relocated. Perhaps it is the classical depth Luciano brings to his gardens that resonates with Cox: marks and forms created against the backdrop of centuries of tradition, and a strong affinity between artist and designer.

KEIICHI TAHARA

BORN
1951

WORKS
Tokyo

Light is an obvious and essential element in our lives, yet to some it remains a constant source of wonder. For Keiichi Tahara it has provided inspiration and delight since the age of five, when he began to experiment with its constantly changing character.

Tahara's later passion for photography as a way of capturing the intangible essence of light grew from this fascination. His early work used the medium to explore feelings and emotion, with a sense of exploration and inquisitive excitement. The old techniques of film processing and developing and the use of silver, which lends great depth to the image, still appeal in his quest to capture mood and intensity.

Not content with simply producing images on paper, Tahara started to explore other surfaces, such as textiles and, most significantly, large slabs of stone. The combination of the expressive subject matter of the transferred image with the patinated distortions, veins and pockmarks of millennia produces intriguing marriages. Many such images were of sculpture, generally figurative, which would through this process in some way be returned to the stone whence it came. Gradually the stone pieces became the sculpture itself, completing the cycle.

In his early twenties Tahara lived in Paris, perhaps attracted by the romantic, bohemian past of this great city. Unable to speak French, and sometimes confined to his apartment out of loneliness, he became fascinated by the way the view from his window changed over the course of the day. The window in turn became an object of fascination, a filter to enable him to communicate with the outside world, and he believes his interest in glass and its transparency as a medium for his photographic work stems from this period.

Tahara created *Baiser* ('Kiss') specially for Luciano's Addison Road garden (pp. 134–49) and its owners, after discussions and the selection of Antonio Canova's sculpture *Psyche Revived by the Kiss of Love* (1793) as the subject matter. The resulting light-capturing box is a series of glass layers, each with a photograph of the work printed on its surface. Sealed within a bronze frame, the glowing images take on a sculptural life of their own. The work's location in the garden captures the imagination and assails the senses almost immediately, albeit in a subtle and seductive way.

The artwork is carefully positioned so that the glass layers refract and catch light throughout the day, glowing and flickering like a ghostly apparition. It is

Sculpture for private garden
(1999), stone and crystal
prism, Saint-Didier, France.

RIGHT *Niwa Garde* (2001),
permanent installation,
black and white marble,
crystal column, European
House of Photography, Paris.

Full-size Art (1996), silver prints on stone and glass, Montreau Park, Montreau, France.

set into the hedge that partitions off the children's play area at the end of the garden, allowing light to enter the installation from front and rear.

Tahara enjoys his involvement with clients and designers, and this shared development has been the catalyst for a changing career. Photography has become his hobby rather than his livelihood, since, in this digital age, film is becoming harder and harder to find. Silvered prints may not be possible for much longer, and that moment of historical technological progress will be lost.

Tahara sees gardens first and foremost as a form of film: surfaces on which light and shadow fall, changing and moving during the daily cycle. His garden for the European House of Photography in Paris (2001; see p. 95) uses contrasting dark and light gravel in direct contradiction, in the manner of a negative. Sculptural elements combine solids, such as rocks, with light-capturing crystal rods and cylinders. The garden as a form of expression remains an essential part of Tahara's creative life and a setting for his sculptural works. He also plays with light itself, throwing beams into the misty sky or focusing them through layers of glass. Reflections also play an important part in these compositions, and his garden

for the Chaumont Festival of Gardens (1998) in the Loire Valley shows this particularly well. A calm eye-level pool with a tiny central island of moss and rocks reflects the trees and surrounding scenery, playing with the viewer's sense of scale.

Tahara is now moving into architecture with the creation of hotels in France and his native Japan. The buildings will, of course, focus on the play of light, translucent surfaces and carefully aligned screens using both natural and artificial materials: an amalgamation of a life's work in sculpture, space and the manipulation of form and light.

Series Torso (1999), photographic emulsion on stone, gold leaf and platinum leaf.

Addison Crescent

ADDISON
CRESCENT
LONDON
2007

PRINCIPAL USE
Private residence

DESIGN
2001; 2006

CONSTRUCTION
2003–2004; 2006–2007

GARDEN AREA
290 sq. m (3100 sq. ft)

For this project in the fashionable district between Holland Park and Kensington, Luciano was engaged in two stages, the first of which involved little more than minor revisions to the terrace following redesign work to the rear facade. Later, when he was invited to redesign the entire garden, he benefited from this earlier knowledge and knew intuitively how the garden should be handled. In turn, the client knew Luciano's work and the way in which he might deal with the space.

Several existing trees dominated the site (which is wide for a city garden), including a large hawthorn, two limes and a magnificent chestnut overhanging from next door; there was also a substantial and mature Virginia creeper (*Parthenocissus quinquefolia*). All would play essential roles in the new design.

To unify the garden Luciano sculpted with hedging, creating tiers on the plot's three boundaries. He used box (*Buxus sempervirens*) for the two lowest levels and yew (*Taxus baccata*) for the highest level, giving a subtle change of colour and texture. The hedging provided a device to frame the garden, but the aim was also to focus the eye on a central sculpture or artwork, which would define the garden as a whole. The play of light along the tops of the hedges is fascinating and one of the most memorable features of this composition. Adding to that and extending the detail into darkness, LED strips supported on hidden aluminium frames between the layers of hedge provide a gentle articulating glow and a dramatic backdrop for entertaining.

Luciano introduced tall Portuguese laurel (*Prunus lusitanica*) behind the hedges at the rear boundary, providing the fourth tier to the hedges and a dark, textured backdrop to the garden as a whole. The gradation from fine texture to coarse and from light to dark green adds depth to the composition.

For the central feature the hedges are interrupted by a plastered wall, smooth and sleek, on which hangs an elegant phosphor bronze sculpture by Nigel Hall. Luciano discovered Hall's work in a gallery belonging to a friend in Majorca, and asked to be introduced. He visited Hall's studio in south London, a double-height space full of incredible models and maquettes, explorations of form, light and shadow to which Luciano was immediately drawn (see pp. 86–89). The client also loved Hall's work and so the commission came about.

The interconnecting cowled loops of *Double Ellipse* stand proud of the smooth wall, allowing shadow to play a part in the piece. They extend across the wall to provide a strong visual link with the horizontal emphasis of the tiered hedges. Below lies a water feature by Andrew Ewing, a reflective surface of shallow water over darker stone, mirroring the sculpture hovering above. At night the bronze is lit from both sides, creating additional shadow patterns. Low jets like candles flush the paving with water, creating movement and sparkle.

The central rectangle of lawn is gently dominated by the main terrace of beige limestone, which forms a link between house and garden. The architect introduced much larger windows to the rear facade, making the role of the terrace much more important. A single step leads from there up to the lawn, creating a homogeneous character and echoing the imposed linearity. Luciano worked closely with the interior designer and architect in order to maximize the view and connection as one first looks into the garden and then enters from the house.

The terrace provides the main entertaining space, running across the entire garden and furnished with generous Sutherland sofas and a long dining table. The furniture was custom-made for the project, and provided an opportunity to develop ideas already set in train in other commissions. In one detail, carefully turned iroko rings sit over the stainless-steel pins that tie the table together. LED lighting below the step coping and uplighters hidden behind tall clay planters and domes of clipped box subtly wash the floor and walls with light.

On the raised ground floor is a second, much smaller terrace paved in timber deck with a dark basalt insert. A small outdoor fireplace provides a warming focal point, and an elegant black-framed canopy provides shelter from the elements. The boundary walls were rendered to match the rear facade of the extended house, unifying the space. For added privacy, slatted iroko screens were mounted on top of the walls, emphasizing and repeating the linearity of the garden below.

The sculpted forms of the evergreen hedging create a solid sense of permanence in the garden, but in autumn the fiery flashes of crimson Virginia creeper make their presence felt, changing the atmosphere and balance of the garden for a few short weeks. This interweaving of the existing and the new is something that Luciano increasingly appreciates, and he sees it as the distinction between imposing the designer's will on a garden and celebrating its individuality.

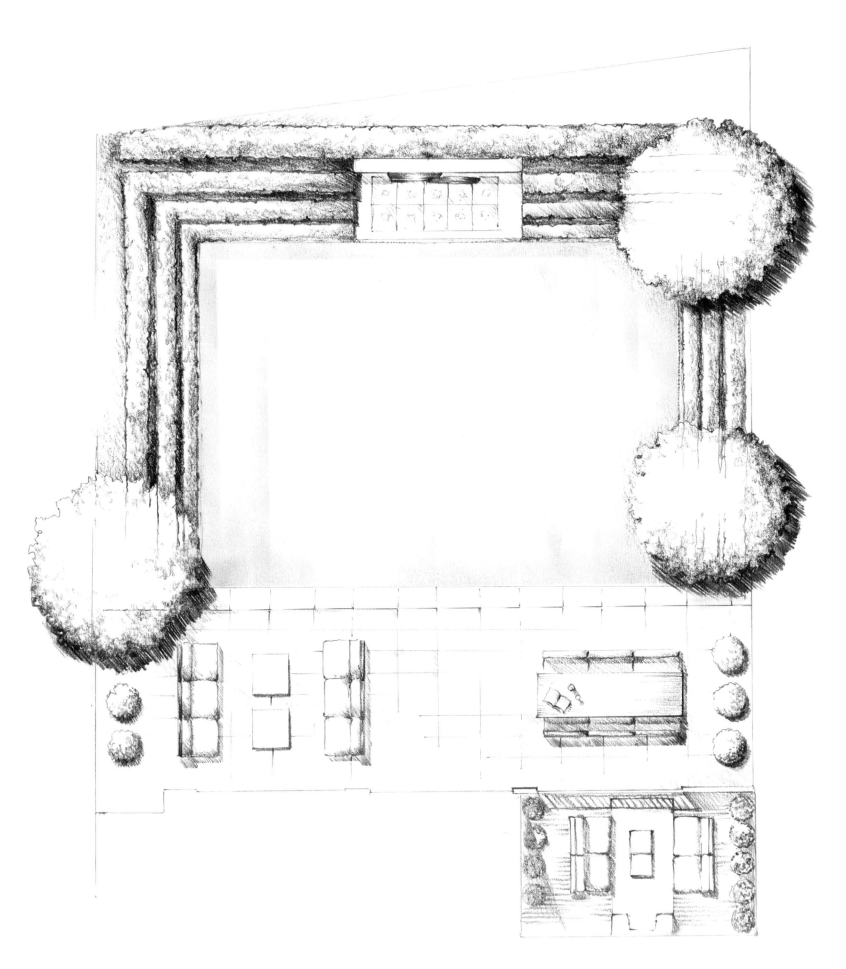

*I see art and garden
as a unified identity, working
as a whole, a richer and
more profound composition.*

OPPOSITE The diagonal view across the garden reveals the relationship between the terrace and the main garden. Nigel Hall's *Double Ellipse* can be seen as the connecting force, set against the borrowed landscape of adjacent gardens.

BELOW Luciano's attention to detail can be seen in his own range of furniture, commissioned for the garden. The stainless-steel connecting rods are covered in iroko washers to create a central divide running the length of the dining table.

The elegance of the garden is best appreciated at twilight, when it is atmospherically lit. An LED provides a continuous cushion of light below the long step, and specially commissioned bronze lanterns articulate the house facade. Uplighters create an ambient glow diffused by carefully positioned containers.

Morocco

MOROCCO
FERME DE SALADIN, OURIKA VALLEY
2009

PRINCIPAL USE
Holiday home

DESIGN
2008

CONSTRUCTION
2008–2009

GARDEN AREA
9150 sq. m (98,500 sq. ft)

Seen from the dry road from Marrakesh, the Atlas Mountains rise out of the plain, casting a rosy glow across the desert terrain. Here Luciano has created a formal oasis and a tranquil retreat that responds to the fascinating light of Africa.

The client, for whom Luciano had previously designed a small London garden, had selected a new property as an escape from a frantic and physically contained London life. The house is set in an ancient olive grove planted on a grid. This sense of order appealed to Luciano, especially since it was created by such venerable and characterful trees, and – inspired by the work of Fernando Caruncho in Spain – he set about using it as the linchpin of the garden. The scale of the plot allowed this 'big idea' to take shape as a single treatment that would respect the ancient groves but inject new vigour into the landscape.

The resulting design forms a large-scale parterre of *Pennisetum alopecuroides*, with 14,000 plants ordered in large terracotta-edged squares separated by wide lawned walkways. Other squares are planted with thousands of Moroccan roses, which fill the air with evening perfume and create blocks of warm colour, searing in the hot, dry air. The silky, light-capturing grasses cast deep shadows or ripple like a silvered sea on which roses seem to float, caught between the gauzy grass and the lifted crowns of the ancient olives.

Throughout the garden there are opportunities to catch these glorious moments: destinations within the ordered grid. Simple, rhythmical paving in terracotta brick or tadelakt (a local material resembling a smooth plaster) provides a warm backdrop for various luxurious but casual seating spaces, decorated with low-level lights with specially made lantern covers, shade-giving steel trellises and pergolas. A cabana next to the swimming pool offers shade and shelter, a cool oasis within the larger garden. The dining area close to the house is protected from the fierce sun by a shaded timber pergola, and elsewhere a fireplace for cooler evenings creates an outdoor living space.

Luciano playfully mixes the local vernacular with select pieces from London. Rugs were bought in the local souk, and old terracotta oil jars provide incidental sculptural forms. Some of the furniture was commissioned from nearby artisans in rust-coloured steel or tadelakt, decorated with colourful cushions. The pool, part of the existing scheme, is finished with glowing, almost iridescent fish-scale tiles, a local speciality. The sharply detailed overflow slot in the paving contrasts with the handmade pool tiles, in a microcosm of the entire garden. Since there was

a language barrier with local craftsmen, contractors and artisans, much of the work was agreed through the production of samples, which allowed the necessary quality control.

The planting similarly fuses European and African ideas. The climate is too hot and dry for box, but plumbago (*Plumbago auriculata*) and pomegranate (*Punica granatum*) were used for low hedges and cushions of foliage. Although the roses and *Pennisetum* are widely used and grow well in this region, individual specimens are more common than massed plantings, which caused some excitement as the garden came together.

Within the main house is a small courtyard planted with orange trees. A white marble water bowl is placed amid tiled pools, on which scented rose petals often float. The guest house is treated in a similar way. An elegant pavilion constructed in steel with a locally typical brown–red finish is planted with roses and jasmine, which fill the air with a fragrance matched in intensity only by the powerful cerise flashes of bougainvillea, which clothes the outer walls.

In a masterstroke, five large concrete bowls created by French artists Les Botta are arranged near the house on a large rectangle of lawn. Although designed for water, they are left empty as sculptural forms, companions to the two giant spinning tops (also by Les Botta) used as a focal point in the main vista of the parterre. The tops' polished upper surfaces contrast with the earth tones and textures of the chiselled concrete, a fitting representation of the cultural integrations in the garden as a whole.

For Luciano there is a sense of separation in the garden, a sacred quality that reminds him of Indian temples and gardens, at once part of the landscape and somehow distinct from it. The entrance gate is the first sign of this separation, but the long drive and glimpses of the formal layout and expansive, glittering parterre reinforce the concept. Mass plantings of agave line the driveway, and clipped hedges focus the eye on the progression through the main door towards the garden beyond.

Accustomed to a greater degree of control in planting than was possible here, Luciano worried about the quality of the completed garden. The development and construction of the whole scheme were relatively short, and he left concerned that the planting would not fill out. He need not have been, for in the benevolent climate the plants flourished and filled out to make the client's first sight a magical scene of rippling, silvery grasses capturing the light and glowing as the evening sun reddened and died.

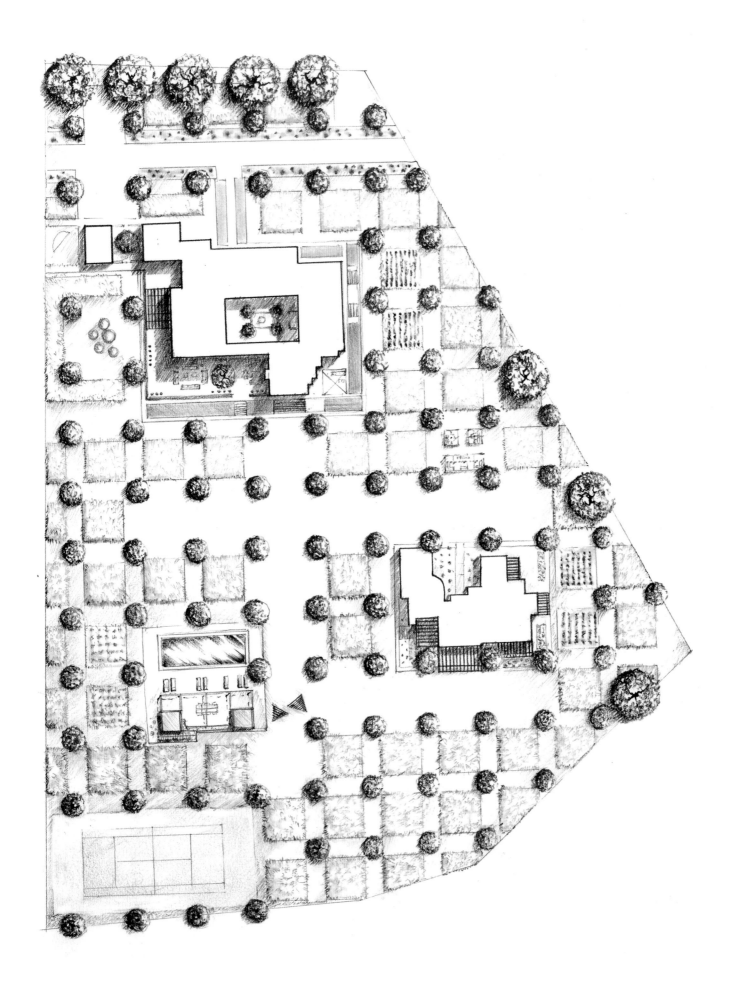

Agave americana (right and opposite) and a more compact agave variety in pots are used en masse around the guest house. Locally sourced containers create an architectural quality. In an unusual detail, the ochre soil is tilled and raked around the planting.

*I fell in love with Morocco
and this garden. The experiences
this profession delivers are
simply magical, and here
I was spellbound.*

THIS PAGE The shady
breakfast terrace extends
into the garden beneath a
canopy. Moroccan leather-
edged rugs break the
surface of the paving, and
the glow of morning light
plays on the wall beyond.

PAGES 126–27 Les Botta's
giant spinning tops play
with the garden's sense
of scale.

The brimming swimming pool maximizes the shimmering reflections of the olive trees and the glowing sky, in the manner of an oasis. The pool house and its pergola provide a backdrop to the sunloungers, designed and commissioned by Luciano.

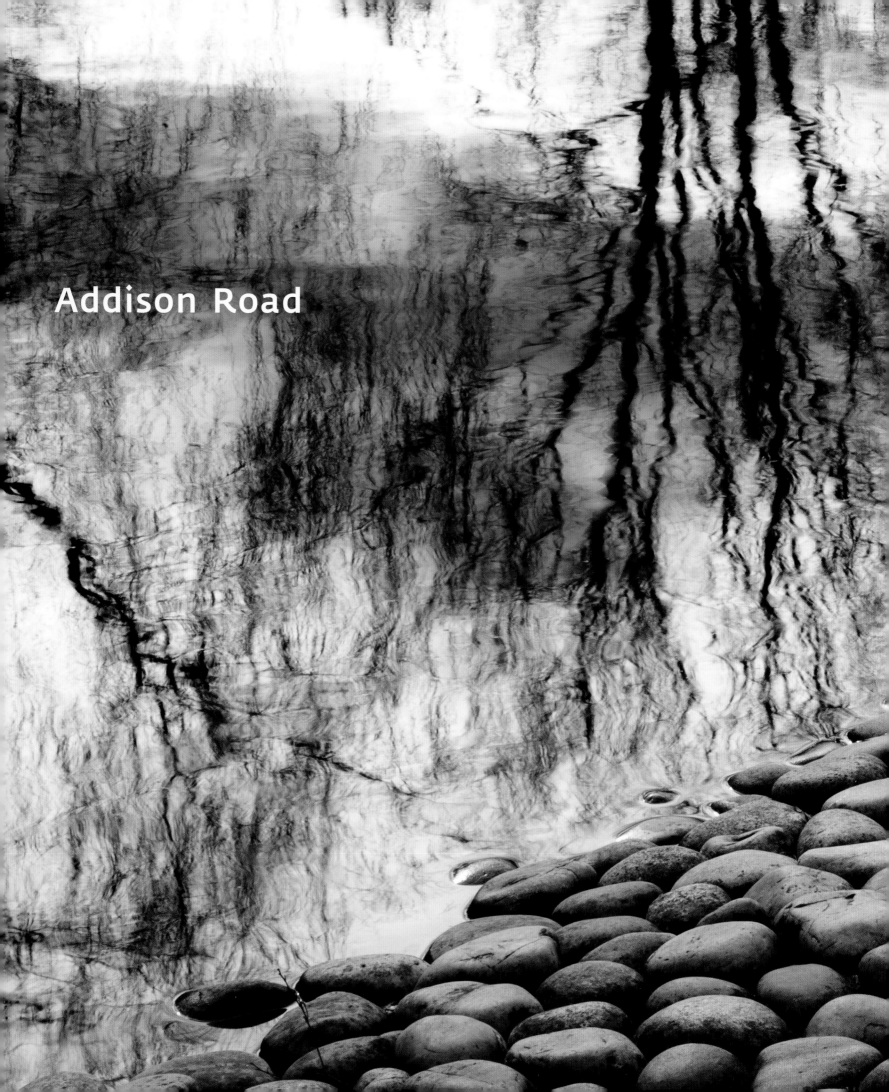

Addison Road

ADDISON ROAD

LONDON

2006

PRINCIPAL USE
Private residence

DESIGN
2005

CONSTRUCTION
2005–2006

GARDEN AREA
610 sq. m (6600 sq. ft)

Many of Luciano's clients employ him again when they move house. The owners of this garden certainly knew who to approach when they relocated from Pelham Crescent (see pp. 43–55), and they called Luciano in during the early stages of the refurbishment of the house. At that point the property was being extended to the rear but offered limited and awkward access to the garden. The new terrace and the connection to the interior became the starting point of the design. Limestone paving pushed out at the new lower level into the garden to produce a generous entertaining space with separate dining and lounging areas. For the first time Luciano introduced furniture made to his own design, inspired by such contemporary designers as John Pawson.

The expansion of the terrace across the entire garden creates a dramatic sense of width dominated by a central staircase that rises to the lawn and its simple rectangular court. The side walls were underpinned (since the level was dropped), rendered and planted with mature blocks of yew (*Taxus baccata*). Access to the site was limited by a 1.2-metre-wide (4 ft) pathway, a logistical problem that often makes progress slow and labour-intensive in London gardens. Additional height and privacy were provided for the garden as a whole by the use of woven willow screens along the tops of the walls. Many trees in the garden and in neighbouring gardens were used as an extended backdrop and a framework within which the formal garden was created.

A retaining wall on each side of the terrace steps is masked by a broad hedge of box (*Buxus sempervirens*) trimmed to the same level as the lawn. Although architectural in form, it immediately softens the space, which in the evening is grazed by floor-mounted lights. North African limestone slabs are laid in stack bond with the joints minimized for a subtle, regular grid across the surface. The tall clay pots that stand like sentinels at either end of the terrace are carefully set out on the same grid and diffuse the lighting, which is positioned behind them. The whole composition is controlled by meticulous order, subliminal rather than overt. Such precision and quality are crucial to Luciano, and he always makes a point of discussing the scale of the garden and the location of lights and containers with his suppliers and craftsmen.

The lawn dominates the higher level of the garden, but it is its delicate framing that works to magical effect. Table-pruned planes create an elegant colonnade along either side, their delicate trunks set in limestone gravel, their line reinforced by low hedges of clipped box. Beyond, the boundaries are clothed in taller hornbeam hedging (*Carpinus betulus*), which gives unity to the garden. The illusion of space is increased after dark as the plane trees are lit from below, producing a delicate tracery against a dark screen of foliage.

Although one tree was lost in the excavation of the main terrace, Luciano insisted that an existing *Robinia pseudoacacia* be retained. It gave immediate maturity and height to the garden, as well as capturing light in the fluttering, fine foliage typical to the species.

The hornbeam hedge cuts across the garden at the top end of the lawn to screen a children's play area with a climbing frame, a rose-planted cottage and a trampoline. Despite this foreshortening, the garden feels spacious and generous, and the children love having the chance to visit what feels like a different world.

In the centre of the garden stands a dramatic focal point, a three-dimensional bronze-framed screen of glass layers, each one a separate photograph but with a different exposure, by Japanese artist Keiichi Tahara (see pp. 94–97). The image, of Antonio Canova's *Psyche Revived by the Kiss of Love* (1793), is one of several photographs of classical sculptures that hold a fascination for Tahara, who named the piece *Baiser*. Fleeting and illusory, the image changes and plays in the light as one moves through the garden towards it. Below it is an Andrew Ewing water feature, a reflective surface of water over black granite that expands the impact of the image and its ghostly, shimmering qualities. The effect is sometimes like that of a mirror, sometimes almost like an opening in the hedge; it flickers and changes as day turns into night.

Recessed into the plane colonnades stand two additional sculptures, much smaller but no less fascinating, set on black-granite plinths. They are not immediately obvious as one enters the garden, but are 'discovered' as the main space opens up. The dynamic, Alberto Giacometti-like figures by Nathalie Decoster are captured within bronze circles, at once contained and full of energy. Symmetrically placed, they demand closer inspection, working as fascinating incidents rather than dominant focal points. Uplighting shows the figures and their frames to best effect with subtle shadows that enrich their character.

The scale and proportions of this garden suggest a bold and confident design approach, but the tracery of the table-pruned planes softens and lightens the whole, complementing and imitating the shimmer and the romance of the sculptural photographs to memorable effect.

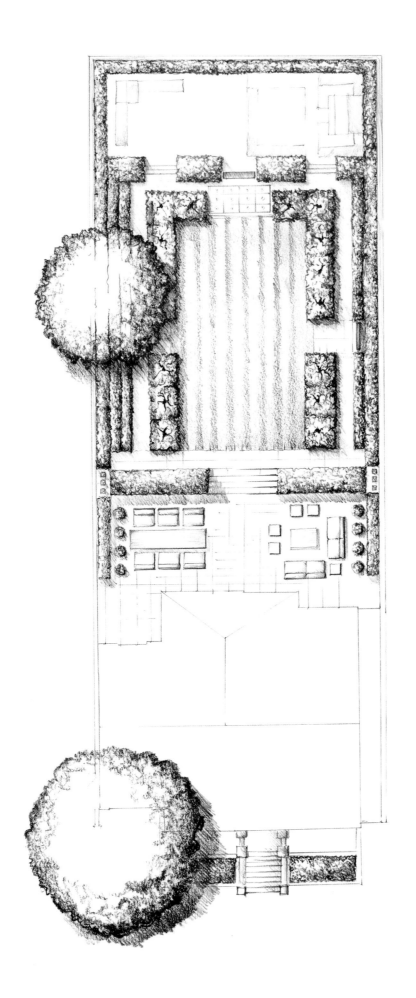

The mystery of the design process still intrigues me: this garden feels much better in reality than I ever thought possible from the design drawings.

An overview shows
the relationship of the
entertaining terrace to
the main garden. Low
box hedges disguise
the retaining wall and
emphasize the steps up to
the lawn. Luciano's own
commissioned furniture
is used for dining (below)
and lounging (right).

The garden contains a range
of spatial experiences, from
the generous seating area
to the narrow gravelled side
allées that run the length
of the garden beneath
the table-pruned planes.
Nathalie Decoster's bronze
is a fascinating focal point.

Kensington

KENSINGTON

LONDON
2003

PRINCIPAL USE
Private residence

DESIGN
2002

CONSTRUCTION
2002–2003

GARDEN AREA
70 sq. m (750 sq. ft)

One of the smallest gardens Luciano has created is also one of the closest to his heart. It is a garden that paved the way for future collaborations with artists and craftsmen and provided a symbolic link between his studies and his life as a successful garden designer.

The garden is located in a quiet street to the south of London's Kensington Gardens, almost hidden away by the surrounding buildings. The original houses date from the middle of the nineteenth century, when the area was known as Kensington New Town, part of the urbanization of west London and covering the former estate of the Vallotton family. Bombing during the Second World War, however, left many parts of London seriously damaged, often scattered sites on which individual houses or small clusters of buildings were ruined and later demolished before being eventually redeveloped. This is one such location where a more modern house has been slotted into an older neighbourhood. During the construction and preparation of the garden the earth yielded huge blocks of masonry from the previous property, echoes of an earlier existence.

The house was under redevelopment when Luciano was contacted by Lucy Eadie, an interior designer with whom he had worked before. She knew the owner, an architect, and felt that Luciano was the right designer for her. The pairing worked well as Luciano and his client discussed the finer details of the scheme and the threshold between house and garden. But the commission suddenly became more meaningful for Luciano when he was presented with a sculptural group by Stephen Cox (see pp. 90–93), *Organs of Action* (1987–88), which the client had recently purchased, to use in the garden.

The work consists of five large granite ovate forms standing on end, representing the mouth, anus, penis, arms and legs: the 'organs of action' of classical Indian philosophy. Influenced by Cox's experience of India, it had been exhibited at the Cass Sculpture Foundation in West Sussex. As Luciano's course director at Inchbald, I regularly took students to the wooded gallery for inspiration, and Luciano immediately recalled the piece and its specific location. The five forms had stood in a shallow depression, a former flint quarry that was now softly graded and turfed, reminiscent of an ancient circle of standing stones.

Inspired and energized by the piece once again, Luciano met the artist and the client to discuss its position, recalling the experience as a dreamlike conversation, since they all shared the same vision and enthusiasm for the project. The rectangular garden was treated like a room and can be seen in its entirety from the main living space to the rear of the property through a wall of sliding glass doors. The interior space gives on to a deck terrace at the same level, and steps descend to the main lawned space, edged with a fine line of limestone paving. The only furniture sits on the deck, backed by elegant clay pots holding clipped lavender (*Lavandula* x *intermedia*).

Simple trellis structures were used on the side walls for privacy, but in front lines of pleached *Pyrus calleryana* 'Chanticleer' stand between two sharply clipped hedges of box (*Buxus sempervirens*), containing the space at a higher level, partly to screen unwanted distractions but also to focus the view from the house on to the end wall. Here the sculptures are displayed in a line facing the house, offering an invitation to enter and explore. A yew hedge (*Taxus baccata*) stands behind to provide a dark but neutral backdrop, and a Japanese cherry – the only plant from the original garden to have been retained by Luciano – overhangs, screening the view of the surrounding properties.

Virtually everything in the garden was craned over the house, a common occurrence with London gardens, which rarely have additional access points to the rear. The workforce and more manageable materials had to come through the building, an especially difficult undertaking since the interior was almost complete at the time of garden construction. In such circumstances good communication is all-important, as logistical problems of this kind can add significantly to the timescales and costs for even the smallest of schemes.

The finished space is intimate, and – as is often the case with small gardens – the finer detail of the design is immediately obvious. The sculptures are tremendously effective in inviting the visitor to explore the space. For the client, the complexities and logistics of the design and construction processes were clearly understood, making the project easier to handle. Luciano himself felt that he had made a connection with the client, as an advocate for his developing career and someone who shared his passion for art and sensitivity to its placement.

The amicable collaboration, including the third member, Stephen Cox, showed Luciano a way to work successfully with other creative minds to enhance and expand the possibilities of his design, and indicated a way forward for the commissions to come.

Art gives my gardens a certain presence, an addictive quality that makes me yearn to work with artists more.

The relationship of this
compact garden with the
house extension, designed
by ACQ Architects, is
formed by the generous
deck. The continuous floor
level provides a direct
view of the sculptures
by Stephen Cox aligned
with the rear wall.
Pleached *Pyrus calleryana*
'Chanticleer' gives privacy,
containing the view.

Site Development

Nurseries and plant material

The gardens of Luciano Giubbilei do not simply happen. Achieving such simple beauty and beguiling elegance involves careful research and a group of suppliers, contractors and specialists who can be relied on to produce the necessary quality over a period of time, not just for a single commission. Many critics and commentators fail to see this aspect of the process for any designer, choosing to review only the final outcome. Although that is, of course, essential, the story of how such results are produced is lost.

As soon as he graduated, Luciano – inspired by his teaching, which had given him a wider view of garden design – started to research plants and the nurseries that would eventually supply him. He knew that the majority of his plant material would come from the great European nurseries of The Netherlands, Germany, Belgium and Italy, but there were also surprises: smaller, specialist family businesses that have worked in plant husbandry for generations. To Luciano these were the jewels, found sometimes by accident as he travelled in search of the hedges and trees that would help to realize his ideas.

While working on an early project in Gloucestershire, Luciano flew to Eindhoven, The Netherlands, in the autumn, and saw huge fields with rows of carefully tended stock laid out like vineyards, the many deciduous species starting to reveal their seasonal colours. His budget for that garden allowed him to use larger and more mature plants than previously, some of them tended and carefully pruned for more than twenty years. That excitement of viewing such horticultural treasures has never left him.

After this first expedition, visits to nurseries on the Continent became a regular and crucial feature of Luciano's professional life. The direct contact with growers allowed Luciano to get to know them and their individual qualities and specialities. He has also developed an understanding of costs that enables him to discuss budgets authoritatively with his clients.

In addition, the growers started to trust Luciano and to show him alternative specimens or new species. As a result, his nursery visits became a way of sourcing new plants or different forms, and started to mould his design thinking. This could be achieved only through familiarization; often he would have lunch or share a drink with the growers, whom he sees as friends and colleagues. Such mutual trust and understanding have a positive impact on Luciano's future gardens.

Through visiting the nurseries, Luciano is also able to gauge the scale of the plants. Although the process might start with emailed photographs, he personally visits each nursery to see the plants himself. For individual specimens it is the size, form and proportion that matter. For hedging or repeated plants, such as pleached or table-pruned trees, he must also think about consistency of form. For his garden in the Boltons he took from the father-and-son-operated Van Roessel Tree Nursery (see p. 167) in The Netherlands, forty-eight trees that had been nurtured for more than twelve years. Luciano loves the timeless quality of this careful tending, likening the process to shopping with a specialist rather than at a supermarket.

Larger operations, such as Bruns and Lorenz von Ehren (both in Germany), are equally amazing, however, with a huge turnover of mature stock and loading and transportation facilities to match. Such mass production is needed, but there is still a place for the smaller, more specialist growers, for example Solitair in Belgium (see p. 168).

Becoming more acquainted with the nurseries and their stock helps Luciano to specify his planting in great detail, enabling him to access the very best stock. He feels Belgium is best for *Buxus*, in either hedge or specimen form. Germany is better for trees, and The Netherlands offers both alternatives. He tends to use nurseries in Italy for Mediterranean stock, such as olives, figs and *Pittosporum*. Plants are normally tagged on each visit to reserve them under his name. On some occasions the tags may be in place for several years, especially if he sees potential in a plant.

On his visits Luciano also discusses his requirements for transportation, although he is always respectful of the growers' advice. The amount of space around each plant and therefore the number carried on each lorry are important considerations. How the plants are lifted and moved is also essential to the health and well-being of these often venerable specimens. This is especially important at the receiving end, where transportation may be limited by access restrictions. In some cases road closures have to be negotiated in order to crane the stock into place, a common occurrence in London gardens, which rarely have clear access. Luciano discusses this in detail with the garden contractor, making decisions based on the most effective way of limiting inconvenience for everyone concerned. Plants may be loaded on pallets in the nursery to make unloading more efficient at the garden. These aspects of

CASE STUDY
Van den Berk Nurseries

This large family-run business has nurseries at St-Oedenrode, near Eindhoven in The Netherlands; Geldern in western Germany; and Rastede in northern Germany. The company has for many years been at the forefront of mechanization, and many tasks are now done by machine to avoid trauma to the trees. At its 280-hectare (690-acre) site in St-Oedenrode (opposite), the company specializes in large trees for avenues, specimen trees and shrubs. The nursery must supply large, uniform batches of trees in perfect condition to clients who do not want to wait for a young tree to reach maturity. The nursery's climate-controlled loading bay ensures that the trees are kept in the best conditions possible while they are packaged and loaded for transportation.

CASE STUDY
Van Roessel Tree Nursery

Boxhead trees (opposite) are standard trees trained by means of specially constructed bamboo frames. At the 10-hectare (25-acre) Van Roessel Tree Nursery, a small family-run business in Berkel-Enschot near Tilburg in The Netherlands, Cees and Thijs van Roessel produce pleached trees, boxheads and screens. In the last picture the nurseryman and adviser Bert van Gils, through whom Luciano buys his plants, discusses requirements with Luciano and a member of the nursery staff.

transportation may add expense to the scheme but will ensure that the plant cargo is delivered in as healthy a condition as possible.

Luciano also provides reassurance and information to the client, who may have forgotten that the planting season is between October and April. Specimens transplanted during this period have a much better chance of survival than those moved in high summer. This timing may not be the most convenient for all concerned, but the plants represent a large investment that must be protected.

Specialist machines lift and prepare root-balled specimens in the nursery, wrapping the roots in wire mesh, which can be fitted with lifting hooks for craning into place. Luciano prefers as much of the handling as possible to be mechanical, since trees are immensely heavy and awkward to move by hand and excessive manhandling can cause damage. Clients can become impatient over the preparation time for these measures, but Luciano always keeps them informed of progress and takes care to explain the details beforehand.

Simply lifting a large stock tree can take two to three hours, not including preparation of the root ball and finer pruning. The skills involved in machine lifting and specimen preparation still fascinate Luciano, and as he watches the nurseryman lifting precious stock or creating the bamboo frames that will guide the growth and pruning of future pleached hornbeam or lime, there is a great sense of careful craftsmanship handed down the generations. These plants might have been under the nursery's care for up to twenty years, a precious investment indeed for Luciano and his clients.

Garden contractors

The individual gardens take time not only to design and detail but also to build. All garden designers need contractors to realize their ideas, as would any architect. These specialist companies stand on the cusps of architecture, engineering and horticulture, bringing a wide range of skills together through their teams. Of greatest importance to Luciano is that these teams share his vision and that there is clear mutual trust.

Luciano requires a positive attitude in his contractors, who must rise to the challenge of his gardens, which rely heavily on finely detailed construction and finishes and high-quality planting, carefully handled. The teams must also work well with the clients, who may see them every day.

The time taken to construct a garden is key for the client. Many are unaware of the intricacies of garden work, and in some cases the demolition of previous gardens can be traumatic. The weather can also play a serious role in delaying progress. Excessive cold may mean that concrete cannot be laid or mortar used for paving joints. Extremes of wet or even hot weather can also have a bearing on the programme. In every scheme unforeseen circumstances will lead to changes in the design or additional attention to detail. Luciano looks for contracting teams that are willing to explore solutions, to bring a positive attitude to a scheme, to share ideas and solutions, and to reduce the impact on the client.

Although he loves the on-site process, Luciano also finds it stressful, especially once the materials appear, as he becomes increasingly protective of their finishes and nervous of mud and dust. He strives to make everyone aware of the big picture and the results he is trying to achieve, but the range of specialists, sub-contractors and suppliers that need to work with the main contractor can make that difficult. Organization and careful planning are prerequisites of the successful gardens he achieves.

Luciano shows the client images of the various stages their garden will go through, to help them see the light at the end of the tunnel. During the process he takes time to show his appreciation of the contractor's skill and patience, often in small ways; perhaps buying chocolate or coffee for the team. He likes to visit regularly to check on progress and discuss the details and any problems.

Mark Gregory, managing director of Landform Consultants, has been a key figure in the production

Solitair Nursery

This specialist nursery in
Loenhout, not far from
Antwerp in Belgium, has
created a plant collection
rather than simply a nursery.
It supplies full-grown trees for
topiary gardens and landscape
gardens, specializing in box
(*Buxus sempervirens*). To Luciano
it is a gallery, displaying an
incredible range of possibilities
for him to browse.

of many of Luciano's gardens. I was aware of the
high quality and great attention to detail of the firm's
work, and so I introduced Gregory to Luciano. The
relationship continues and has been of mutual and
lasting benefit. Gregory assesses each scheme and the
needs of the site very clearly, and will often point out
areas that need particular attention or care. That
positive attitude is evident in Landform's work, and
the company responds well to the challenges of
each design, from the detailing to the all-important
logistics of transportation, road closures and access.

One of the difficulties of the garden-design
profession is the relative isolation of the designer,
especially early in one's career. Gregory and his
team offered that vital support and a wider field
of knowledge to Luciano when he needed it most.
Luciano cherishes those shared times now, relishing
their combined vision and the resulting expansion
of his knowledge.

Early in his career, Luciano visited his sites every
day, fascinated to see his designs taking shape. Now
he visits regularly or sends members of his team,
asking them to photograph and report back in detail.
He still takes time to talk regularly with the site

foreman, ensuring that he is up to date with any
developments. For most schemes, especially those
overseas, he agrees to dedicate a certain time each
month – perhaps four or five days – to the project.
That way he can deal with snags easily, and also
report to his clients. This close involvement of
designer, client and contractor is critical to the success
of each scheme: lines of communication are always
open and the process is made as painless as possible.

Craftsmanship and specialists

Luciano's design philosophy is embodied in each design, but the spaces are also populated by a range of artefacts, pools, crafted materials and furniture. Andrew Ewing is a favourite collaborator, a specialist who works his magic with water to create many of the shallow pools and glistening features that form the focal point of many of Luciano's gardens. The pouring cascades and dark films of water that gave depth and shimmering life to the Laurent-Perrier garden at the RHS Chelsea Flower Show in 2009 (see pp. 176–91) came from Ewing's studio, and his simple sheens of water reflect many of the artworks that Luciano or his clients select.

Ewing floods water over the surface of natural stone to emphasize the grain, or floats a shallow film of water over paving that acts as a lid to a buried water tank. Tiny candle-like jets of bubbling water, lit from below, glimmer after dark and throw light on to surrounding surfaces. Such simple apparitions are technically highly inventive and complex, intriguing in their sense of mystery but refreshing and ever-changing to the eye and ear.

The massive solidity of the sculpted concrete forms created by French artists Serge Bottagisio and Agnes Decoux (Les Botta; see p. 173) provides a totally different dynamic. Elegant containers are a signature of Luciano's gardens, and as well as the massive solidity of Les Botta's forms he likes smoother finishes, which reflect light and create interesting shadows. Luciano frequently uses containers by Atelier Vierkant (see p. 171), a craft-based family company that exploits clay's flexibility to its limit and has transformed the traditional preference for terracotta pots. Luciano describes their tall, elegant containers in shades of grey, black and brown as 'timeless'. In association with lighting these containers create shadows and architectural highlights, or, used as a block, direct the light, their forms silhouetted against an uplit wall. When left unplanted, they are sculptural forms with a beauty and a presence of their own; if planting is used, Luciano prefers clipped box, the weight and density of form of which complements the containers.

Nigel and Mary Chapman of Hode Pottery in Kent (see p. 171) are typical of the traditional approach that Luciano likes so much, producing handcrafted pots of distinction in an unusual biscuit colour. Seeking

CASE STUDY
Atelier Vierkant (opposite)

Luciano first saw Atelier Vierkant's planters at a show in Paris and was immediately filled with a great enthusiasm, envisaging how the simple, elegant objects could complement his designs. Their subtle tones and simple funnel forms (opposite; see also pp. 162–63) reinforce Luciano's calm, contemporary style, and he has formed a successful partnership with the Belgian company. Although he might send drawings or specify sizes, each piece is handmade by touch rather than by accurate measurement. Luciano is firm friends with the three people who make the company work: Willy and Annette Janssens and Pierre Vanherrewege. He admires the combination of a traditional approach with new ideas, and the high-quality design and craftsmanship of every piece.

CASE STUDY
Hode Pottery (right)

Nigel and Mary Chapman of Hode Pottery produce unusual containers in their workshop in Kent. Using stoneware clay (right), Nigel first throws and works the base of the pot, then adds 10-centimetre-wide (⅓ in.) strips of clay in stages in a process that can take up to three weeks. The clay must be allowed to dry as any moisture will explode the pots in the kiln. The pots are so large that this is the only way in which they can be produced. The first firing creates earthenware and the second vitrifies the pots into stoneware at very high temperatures, ensuring that they are frostproof.

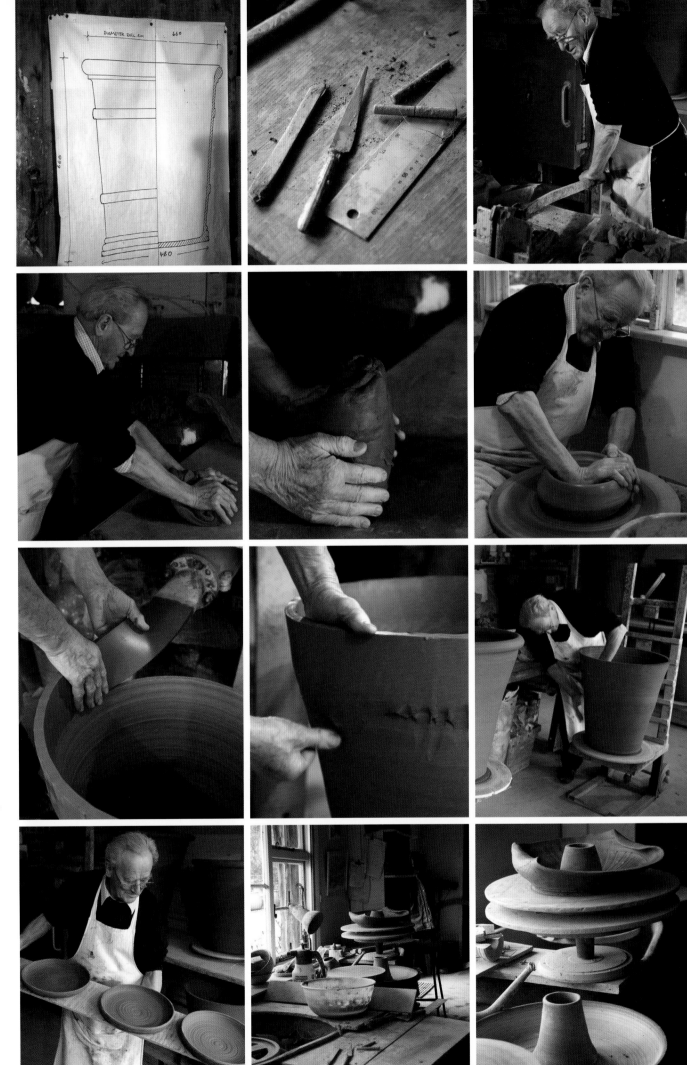

Serge Bottagisio and Agnes Decoux form the partnership Les Botta, which is based in Dému in southern France. They layer terracotta and concrete, tearing away the latter to reveal the warmer tones of the terracotta underneath. The textured lines that result create movement and demand an exploratory touch, articulating the surfaces of these monumental forms. Luciano chose their bowls and spinning tops for the garden in Morocco (see pp. 114–33), and the silent forms underpin the calm and reflective quality of the place.

containers of architectural and sculptural character to help make his gardens distinctive, Luciano first commissioned Nigel in 1997, during the development of the Harcourt Terrace garden (see pp. 14–16). Hode Pottery's 'Long Toms' have graced many of his gardens since that project. The Chapmans' warmth and hospitality to Luciano on his various visits remind him of his Italian upbringing, and the sharing of a love of simple food and good company.

Now in his eighties, Nigel still creates pots in his garden workshop. As one watches him at work, it is clear how much effort is involved, and with two twelve-hour firings for each container the embodied time adds up. Only two pots can be fired at a time, and with as many as twenty-five pots required for Luciano's larger gardens, each commission represents an enormous investment of time, energy and skill. The Chapmans have chosen to retain a small-business approach rather than to expand, meaning that their lives and their business are perfectly interwoven. This carefully controlled craftsmanship, which fulfils the creative need but does not grow out of hand, perfectly suits Luciano's own experience and philosophy.

Luciano regularly uses the specialist firm English Hurdle to weave handmade screens for privacy, in particular in his London gardens. The craft of creating woven barriers and screens from willow or withies has changed little in the last 1000 years. The business, run by the Hector family in the Somerset Levels, is based at their farm, which is surrounded by coppiced willow. The fine, springy stems are harvested and woven by hand to create the necessary tautness and pattern. Each craftsman signs his own work. The willow coppices themselves have become a valuable wildlife habitat, which is sustained by this method of farming.

To furnish his gardens Luciano combines two approaches. His early searches for pieces of distinction eventually led him to the firm of Sutherland in the USA; he then began to create his own range of garden furniture to suit the scale and ethos of his designs more directly, and regularly uses this for his garden commissions.

The link to Sutherland came early in Luciano's career, as he searched for furniture that would provide the connection between the interior and the garden. Research led him to David Sutherland's elegant furniture, which is for permanent outdoor use but looks just as much at home indoors. This furniture has become something of a signature for Luciano. Built

from teak and upholstered with tough weatherproof textiles, these pieces exude luxury and quality, and their generous proportions are ideal for the spacious terraces Luciano creates.

A great admirer of the way minimalist architects incorporate furniture into their simple, precise schemes, Luciano started to design and produce his own range of furniture, with the aim of preserving the atmosphere he seeks to create. Comfort is an aspect of his design thinking that touches everything he does, and, above all, he wanted the furniture to be comfortable so that his clients could enjoy their gardens. The craftsmen he uses are highly skilled and experienced, with a high level of respect for the qualities of the materials they use; such respect and knowledge, Luciano feels, help the pieces speak for themselves. The high-quality hardwood iroko they use in the Oxfordshire workshop comes from sustainable plantations; it is machined from long lengths of solid timber 80 millimetres (3 in.) thick to keep the number of joints to a minimum, giving the impression of a seamless, 'poured' surface that is nevertheless alive with the warmth and organic qualities of wood.

The process of fitting all these elements together to make the finished garden is a complicated one, and was seen in its most intensive form during the three-week construction of Luciano's Laurent-Perrier Garden at the RHS Chelsea Flower Show in 2009. Teamwork at all times and constant consultation with colleagues and the designer are crucial, and the series of photographs overleaf shows just how it was done (for the finished garden, see pp. 176–91).

Champagne producer Laurent-Perrier, the sponsor for Luciano's garden at the Royal Horticultural Society's Chelsea Flower show in 2009 (see pp. 176–91), requested a design that was both sophisticated and understated. The process of producing a garden for the show is relatively short, and good planning is crucial if the garden is to be looking at its best for the week of the show in late May. Some months before construction started (three weeks before the show) Luciano and his team were finalizing the design and details with the contractor, Crocus, after which mock-ups and samples of the garden features were produced. Meanwhile the plants were being nurtured in shade tunnels and glasshouses, being held back or encouraged so that they would be perfectly in flower for the judging. Once construction began, the team worked hard to realize Luciano's meticulous plans, craning trees carefully into position, laying stone for paths and walls and positioning the artwork and plants.

Chelsea

LAURENT-PERRIER GARDEN

RHS CHELSEA FLOWER SHOW, LONDON 2009

PRINCIPAL USE
Show garden

DESIGN
2008

CONSTRUCTION
2009

GARDEN AREA
225 sq. m (2400 sq. ft)

In 2009 Luciano made waves at the world-famous RHS Chelsea Flower Show, the Royal Horticultural Society's great spring showcase, which takes place each May in the grounds of the Royal Hospital, Chelsea, on the banks of the River Thames. Contractors have three weeks to build display gardens on the football pitches for the week-long show, after which they are dismantled.

In 2008 Tom Stuart-Smith, who had previously designed show gardens for the champagne house and long-standing Chelsea garden sponsor Laurent-Perrier, proposed Luciano as his successor. Despite initial reservations about the show, Luciano felt a wave of enthusiasm once he had visited Stuart-Smith's garden, realizing that this was a huge opportunity to communicate with a much wider audience, and to work with a key sponsor that shared his ideals and aspirations. The time felt right to design his first show garden.

Stuart-Smith suggested that Luciano might stay true to his work and create a garden without flowers, but Luciano decided to embrace them and take the opportunity to develop a new palette of plants, intending to convey the calm spirit and atmosphere of the garden through the three-dimensional forms of the planting. All show-garden designers must submit a written plan describing their endeavours; their gardens are firstly assessed and then judged on this information. The process was a revelation for Luciano, allowing him to rationalize and reflect on his composition objectively, and he would recommend it to anyone involved in the design process.

The process of creation began almost as soon as Laurent-Perrier had agreed to the scheme, and Luciano immediately benefited from the support of the Crocus contracting team, which has been producing successful Chelsea gardens for more than a decade. He is full of respect and gratitude for the care and attention to construction and planting detail shown by the team led by Mark Fane, whom he met regularly to keep an eye on progress. As the build started Luciano visited the showground, anticipating that he might call in from time to time, but from the first day he was hooked, effectively working from the garden rather than his office. His love affair with garden-making was rekindled, and the magic of the transformation caused him to reflect on his whole experience so far.

As with all Chelsea gardens, Luciano's design would be seen from two directions, and only from its boundaries. From the longest side of the rectangular site, a long colonnade comprising three separate blocks of pleached hornbeam (*Carpinus betulus*) framed views into the main space. A simple gravel surface beneath the trees lightened the shade, broken only by sheets of water falling from sculpted bronze rills into openings between the blocks of trees.

From the shorter side of the garden the colonnade also framed a long view to the back wall, the site of *Big Bite*, a wall-mounted sculpture in Cor-ten steel by Nigel Hall, seen in relief against a reredos of unfilled Tuscan travertine. This material was sourced close to Siena, clearly linking the fabric of the garden with Luciano's ancestral territory. The dark stone for the pools came from Verona, the centre of Italy's stone industry. A second view from this boundary looked down the centre of the garden, framed by the hornbeam pleaching on one side and a stepped hedge of box (*Buxus sempervirens*) and yew (*Taxus baccata*) on the other. The design also took advantage of the high pleaching used in Ulf Nordfjell's garden on the neighbouring site. The result was a cathedral-like space, architectural in its three-dimensional form but green and living. The yew hedge was left untrimmed for a soft outline, which caught the light and contrasted with the brighter green of the lower box.

A pathway running the length of the garden also led to a central seating and relaxation area furnished with low Sutherland sofas and screened with the tall, rustling grass *Calamagrostis* x *acutiflora* 'Karl Foerster'. In front of and beyond the grass screens jewel-like flowers floated in a dark sea of frothy bronze fennel (*Foeniculum vulgare* 'Purpureum') lit with flashes of *Deschampsia cespitosa* grass: deep amethyst-purple irises 'Superstition' and 'Black Swan', sapphire-blue *Salvia nemorosa* 'Caradonna' and the ruby flashes of *Astrantia major* 'Claret' and A. 'Hadspen Blood' against blowsy *Paeonia* 'Buckeye Belle'.

In contrast, the muted tones and textures of the travertine made a simple geometry of the pathways and walls. A brown leatherstone was used as the base for the shallow pools, and travertine was again used, to create a series of low seats and water blocks that provided an alternative social space at the far end of the garden.

Sunlight breaking through clouds would cause the colours and textures of the garden as a whole to flicker suddenly into life, with clear shadows setting the drama in high relief. The sculpture also changed dramatically, creating its own shadows against the monolithic wall, pulling the huge circle into sharp focus. Below, the transformation was reflected in a shallow pool. Luciano and Andrew Ewing collaborated on the water features, which contributed to a subtle life force within the garden, offering a gentle splashing sound and cooling the warm spring air.

Assessment began on the Sunday prior to the week of the Chelsea show. Although Luciano was proud of the quality of the garden, the process of judging for a coveted medal was a daunting prospect: he knew the garden had to be more than perfect. Judging took place on the following day, by which time the garden was in peak condition. That day is also devoted to press and media coverage and to the royal visit. Her Majesty The Queen comes to the Chelsea Flower Show each year and tours selected gardens, and Luciano was proud to show her, the Prince of Wales and the Duchess of Cornwall around his garden. The medals were conferred the following morning, and with some relief Luciano awoke to the glory of a gold medal coupled with huge pride and a great sense of achievement after eleven years as a designer.

The excitement of Chelsea comes as a series of crescendos, and once the show opened to visitors Luciano was amazed at their overwhelmingly positive response to the garden. They seemed to understand his concepts entirely, an endorsement that came against a backdrop of phenomenal press and media coverage, including much in his home country, where the story made front-page headlines. A particularly poignant comment came from a member of the Laurent-Perrier dynasty, who remarked on the way in which light and shadow revealed the true character of the garden, something that Luciano strives for in all his work, but especially in this garden.

At the end of the show, the gardens are dismantled within days, an unusual occurrence in the garden world and one that many designers find hard to bear. For Luciano it brought philosophical reflection on what he had achieved since starting his career, and a certain amount of soul-searching. What became apparent was the sense of a new direction, the challenge of designing with colourful flowering perennials, renewal in his design work and the rediscovery of a vigour and a passion for garden design that he remembered from his studies at Inchbald. As for the Chelsea Flower Show, he had been bitten by the bug and was already looking forward to the opportunity to design there again.

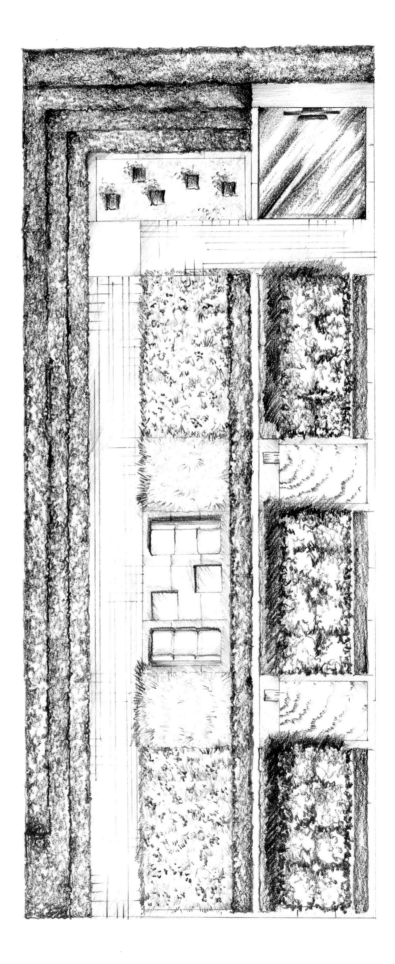

PREVIOUS PAGES AND FAR RIGHT Light falls on the surfaces of the layered hedges, which provide a controlled setting for the diaphanous planting.

OPPOSITE The textured central planting, contained by strict lines of yew and box hedging, is seen through the pleached hornbeam *allée*.

RIGHT The glowing colours of *Paeonia* 'Buckeye Belle' shine through the purple spears of *Salvia nemorosa* 'Caradonna'.

BELOW *Deschampsia cespitosa* provides a froth of light-catching flowers to support the velvety blackcurrant petals of *Iris* 'Superstition'.

The access to a wider public across the world provided me with a huge lift: the opportunity to express what I do on an international stage.

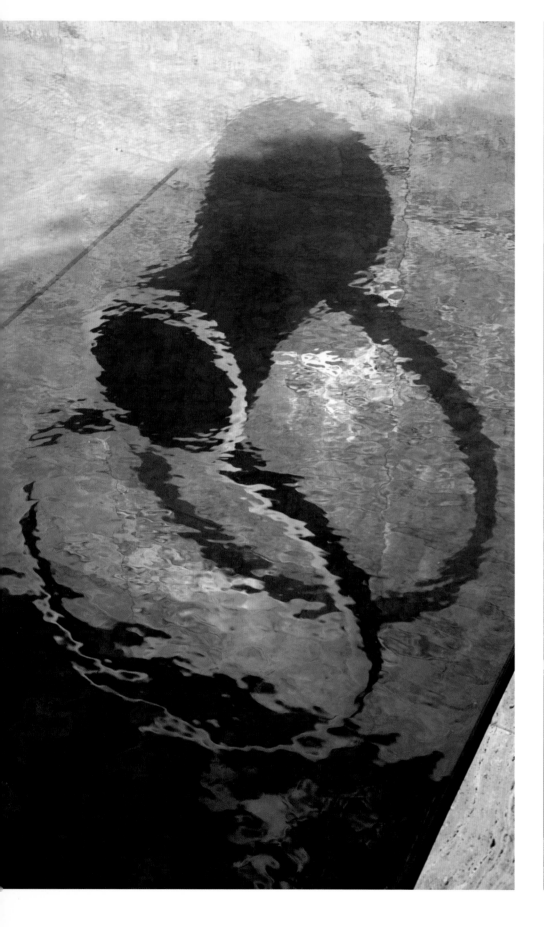

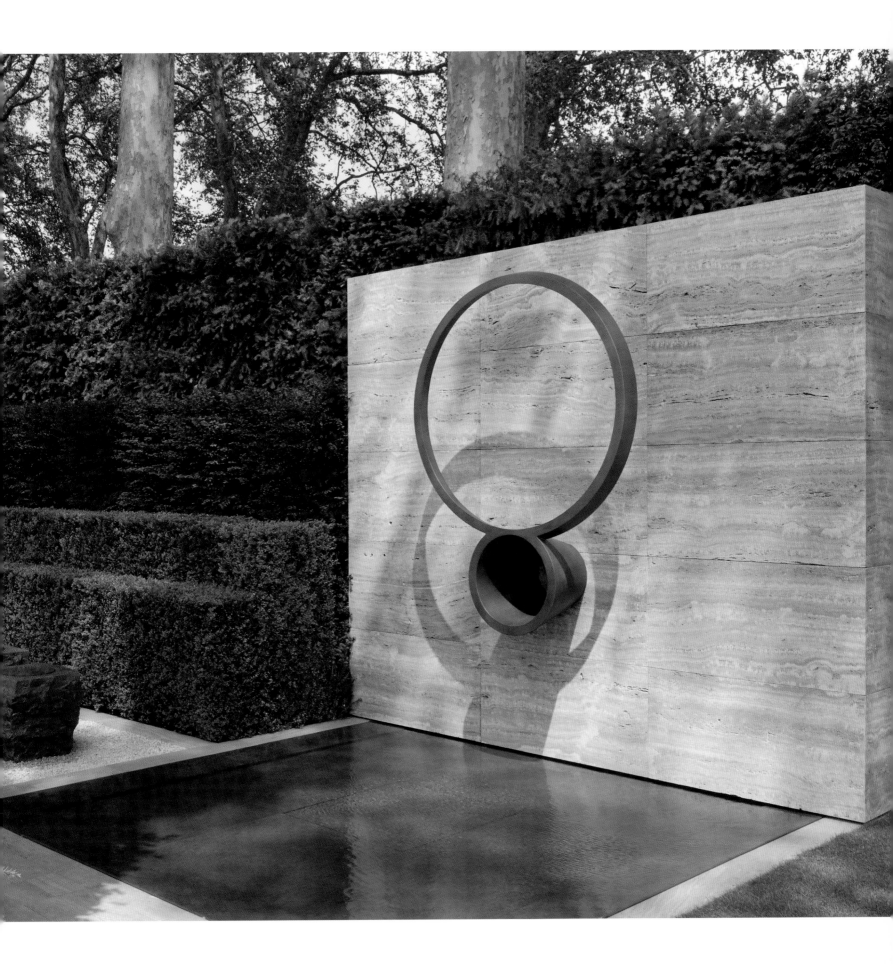

Light plays on the textured travertine, and elegant patinated bronze spouts throw the water clear of the stone blocks. The dark brown leatherstone is enhanced by the water that spills continuously over it, and contrasts with the meticulously laid paving.

Notting Hill

NOTTING HILL

LONDON
2005

PRINCIPAL USE
Private residence

DESIGN
2004

CONSTRUCTION
2004–2005

GARDEN AREA
130 sq. m (1400 sq. ft)

Notting Hill is pervaded by the grandeur of its older houses, and for this client – a designer – the architecture of Thomas Allom (1804–1872) proved irresistible, capturing the confident sway of the Victorian age. Luciano had met her during the build of his Boltons garden in 2001 (see pp. 29–41), and remembered her interest in the fine detail and finish of that garden as it came to completion. By 2004 she had a new house to develop and refurbish, and she called Luciano in to work his magic.

The house's elegant rear facade, with its generous bay window and white stucco finish, was for Luciano a key feature, providing a dramatic backdrop to the garden. The main reception room is slightly raised above the ground, its bay providing a long and intensely green view through the garden into the communal space beyond. This feeling of distance and the sheltering boscage give an illusion of scale and creates in this private space a quality of refuge and containment.

The communal garden resolved a problem many smaller London gardens raise for young families, that of space for children to play in and explore, and left the smaller private space for family entertainment and relaxation. Luciano knew, however, that this garden would need to relate to the large, mature trees of the setting and the Victorian grandeur of the house.

The result is a garden within a garden, a sophisticated place to which the family can withdraw from the more public shared area. The outdoor room, which allows comfortable social discourse and relaxed but luxurious entertaining, was central to the design and to the needs of the family, and forms a bridge between the house and its context.

Limestone paving divides the garden and links the house with the gate into the communal area. A lawn forms the softer half of the garden; circulation and entertaining occupy the other half. The gate was Luciano's idea and was inspired by archival drawings of the house, echoing the ornate wrought-iron detailing popular when it was built. The gate ensures privacy and provides a boundary but allows the view to continue virtually uninterrupted.

The garden walls were rebuilt and rendered in a neutral colour, then softened by planting. Yew (*Taxus baccata*) frames the fireplace and creates a sense of depth with its dark, uniform texture. Only one element was retained: a 4-metre-high (13 ft) privet hedge (*Ligustrum*). It was cut hard back to increase the available space, and as a result took on a new lease of life with much tighter branching and foliage cover. It forms a mature backdrop to two lower steps of box (*Buxus sempervirens*) that run parallel to it. As light

falls on these contrasting surfaces they are rendered graphic and architectural, and the original hedge is drawn into the garden as a key element.

In the outdoor room, which occupies the paved portion of the garden, table-pruned *Acer platanoides* creates a dappled ceiling over the polished-concrete fireplace and central seating area, providing privacy and shelter. The linear nature of the canopy echoes the pathway below and guides the view into the garden beyond the boundary. The fireplace forms both a welcoming gesture and a focus for the seating area. The play of light here – lively shadows during the day and dancing flames at night – creates a natural and easy centrepiece, full of movement and quiet vitality.

The furniture was selected for its sleek and low but comfortable lines: long, three-seater Sutherland sofas and delicate stainless-steel occasional tables from BowWow. The tables are easy to move and reflect the dancing shadows and flickering flames. Rather than individual chairs, the dining table has benches, which can be stored underneath to save space. A small cooking area near by enables the family to decamp completely into the garden in warm weather.

The simple rectangle of lawn balances the space, providing an area for play and relaxation and acting as a canvas on which the changing light and shade patterns play. The path and terrace are paved in pale limestone enlivened by rectangular beds of limestone gravel around the tree trunks, creating a softer texture.

After dark the garden comes alive with theatrical lighting and flickering fire, taking on the proportions and qualities of a room within a garden setting. Uplighters recessed into the paving illuminate the delicate foliage canopy, and candles lend a more relaxed character. As a composition, Luciano feels, the design could have nothing added or removed without losing its balance. The garden certainly has an assured tranquillity and a timeless sense of confident elegance that belie its efficient functionality, and that is surely part of its success.

Here, I wanted to create a space as a retreat, a green experience that would act as an outdoor living room.

The link between the
interior spaces and the
garden is an essential
consideration for Luciano.
The view runs out over the
stepped bridge, through
the garden and into the
communal space beyond.

The polished plaster fireplace provides the focus both for the garden and for the main entertaining space, next to the central path. The flames dance through an asymmetric sculpture silhouetted against the flickering light, and the table-pruned canopies overhead catch the subtle uplighting (overleaf).

Barcelona

BARCELONA

SPAIN
2008

PRINCIPAL USE
Private residence and showroom

DESIGN
2004–2005

CONSTRUCTION
2007–2008

GARDEN AREA
220 sq. m (2350 sq. ft)

In 2004 Luciano was asked by one of Spain's most celebrated jewellery designers to design a roof garden in Barcelona. She had bought a penthouse apartment opening on to the third-floor garden in the Banco Urquijo, a block by one of Spain's leading post-war architects, José Antonio Coderch (1913–1984). A design-and-build company was responsible for the entire refurbishment, and in many ways this 'one-stop shop' approach made the project more tenable, since Luciano would be working remotely from London.

Luciano's first visit revealed a jungle: existing planting had been allowed to choke the space, making it difficult to appreciate. Little could be placed by the huge floor-to-ceiling windows since they were operable, and the complex floor plan – brought about by the many bays and projections, designed to maximize natural light – made a clean, structured geometry difficult. Reading the space as one volume inside and out unlocked Luciano's inertia. As a result, the architecture of the garden flows past and through the apartment, uniting the two in a way that would, he feels, have made Coderch happy. This transparency in the spatial treatment is crucial to the success of the design.

The garden features stand back towards the parapet, creating a series of interlocking views that enrich the experience from inside the apartment. Searching for a suitable structural plant, Luciano realized that the climber *Trachelospermum jasminoides* would be perfect. Tolerant of shallow, dry soils, it suits rooftop conditions, where soil must be contained and weight is restricted. Its tiny cream flowers also infuse the space with an intense fragrance.

The project spanned four years from first contact, a factor that helped in the search for plants. Luciano contacted Rolando Innocenti, a specialist nursery in Pistoia, Italy, to explore the creation of planting blocks. The nursery made steel frames that could be fixed into planting containers, and nursed the *Trachelospermum* over the course of a year into the forms and density that would create suitable screens. Eventually the plants were moved to a nursery in Gerona, closer to Barcelona, to acclimatize. Transplanted into place as mature features 2.5 metres (8 ft) high, they had instant and defining impact on the garden: structural screens following the architectural rhythm.

Although the views from the roof terrace are extensive, they are not always remarkable, and the climbers provided a way of controlling them, allowing important glimpses of the city and screening unwanted distraction. Privacy was assured in the process. The garden comes alive after dark, however, when the city lights lead out to sea in a sparkling display, echoed by the subtle lighting within the apartment.

As part of the refurbishment, the windows and doors were replaced with bronze powder-coated aluminium. For coherence, Luciano adopted the same finish for the exterior lighting, pergola and planters. The paving of black Spanish basalt echoes this darker tone and allows the glossy green foliage of the *Trachelospermum* to shine, contrasted with tightly clipped domes of box. The charcoal-grey Spanish stone has a leathery finish, a soft grain that works well over such a large expanse. It is partnered by oiled ipe decking, which is used especially in the seating areas and bedroom terraces to provide a warmer surface under foot.

An elegant pergola runs along one side, giving height and a sense of light enclosure to the garden and providing a defined seating space focused on an outdoor fireplace in Venetian stucco, which matches the pergola in height. The fire can be controlled from inside the apartment, as can the protective awnings, which work individually for each bay of the pergola, providing shade against the heat of the sun by day and shelter from the cooler evening breezes. Delicate and transparent cord-drum occasional tables counteract the weight of the Sutherland chairs. The fire also provides a focal point from inside the apartment, playing on the sense of confusion between interior and exterior. At one end of the pergola, tall black clay pots planted with domes of box provide a focus; at the opposite end, a finely tooled iroko screen filters light and protects the terrace from wind, completing the sense of subtle enclosure. The diffused view of Barcelona beyond provides a tantalizing sense of context, but it is the elegant shadow-play that provides the main attraction as the sun tracks across the terrace.

A large curtained daybed mirrors the architecture of the pergola but is invisible from the apartment, hidden behind the fireplace. As a result the bed – a playful surprise when the garden is explored – offers privacy and a true place of escape.

This carefully crafted design, which respects the integrity of the elegant architecture, was refined with the detailed and enthusiastic involvement of the client. The result is magical, Luciano feels, especially when the lighting comes into play. Recessed LED strips skirt the planting boxes, making them appear to float, and silhouetted forms and dramatic pools of light produce enticing glimpses from every window. By day the sense of containment by the tall blocks of planting is no less exciting in this cool and evocative escape from the lively city below.

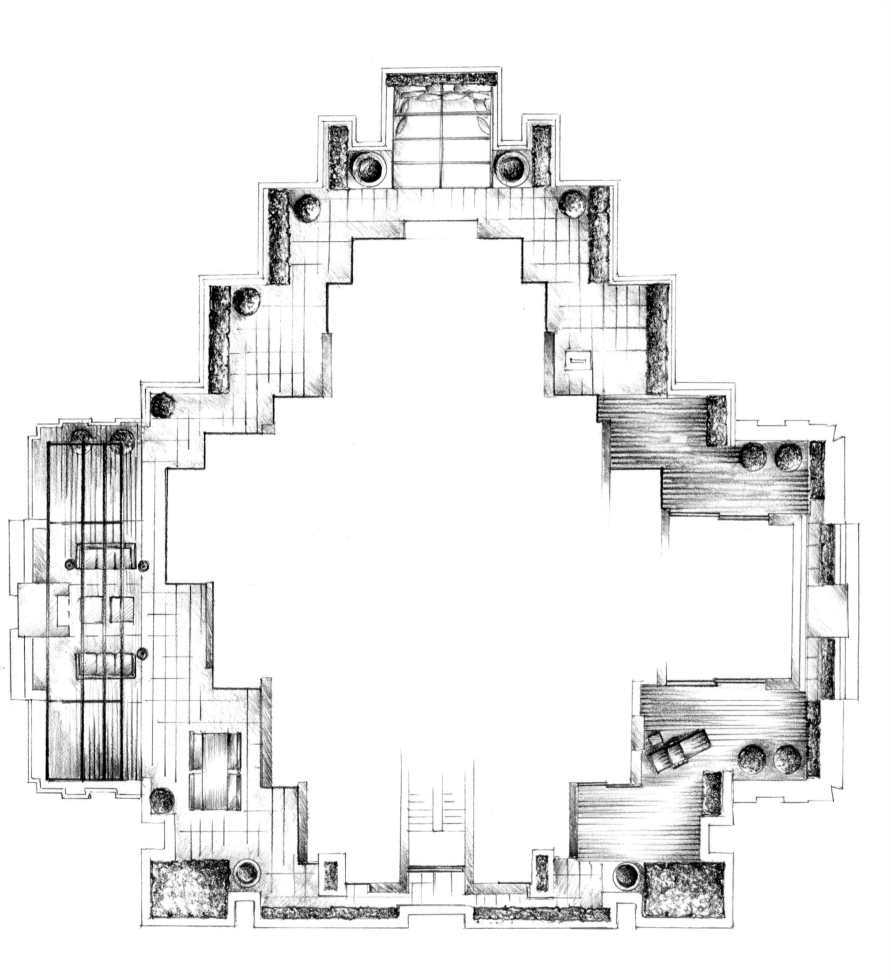

The garden creates magical illusions: the play of light and shadow confuses the eye as to what might be indoors and what outdoors.

PREVIOUS PAGES, AND
OPPOSITE A screened,
architectural pergola
creates outdoor rooms
shaded from the sun,
allowing entertaining
to spill out of doors.

BELOW The glass walls
create a single living space,
the division between
outside and inside blurred
and incidental.

The fragrant climber *Trachelospermum jasminoides* is used as hedge-like blocks of texture, creating tightly clipped but soft screens of glossy green foliage. These living walls protect and enclose the roof terrace, creating a shady enclosure and allowing dappled light on to the textured floor.

Discreet uplighters throw light on to the living screens, creating a sense of indoor space on the terrace. The reflected light, supplemented by downlighters, is diffused over the fireside seating, and emphasizes the forms of the terracotta pots.

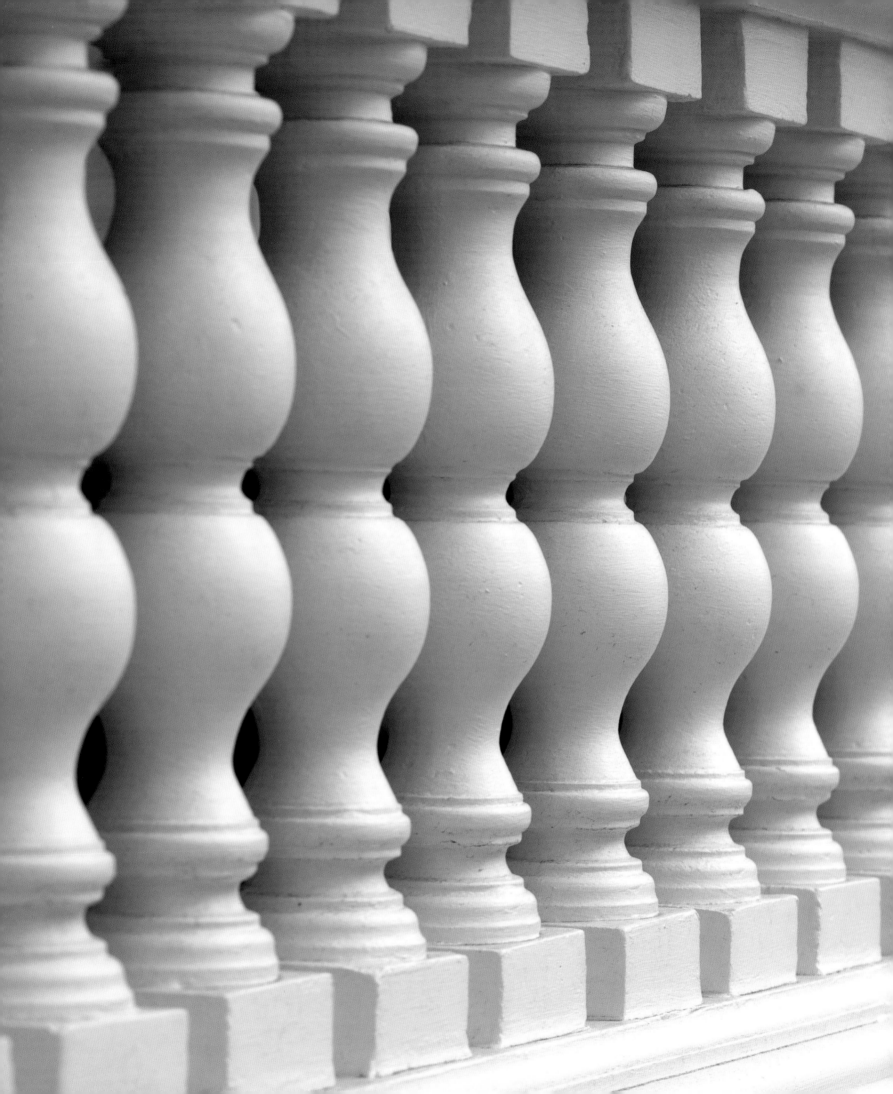

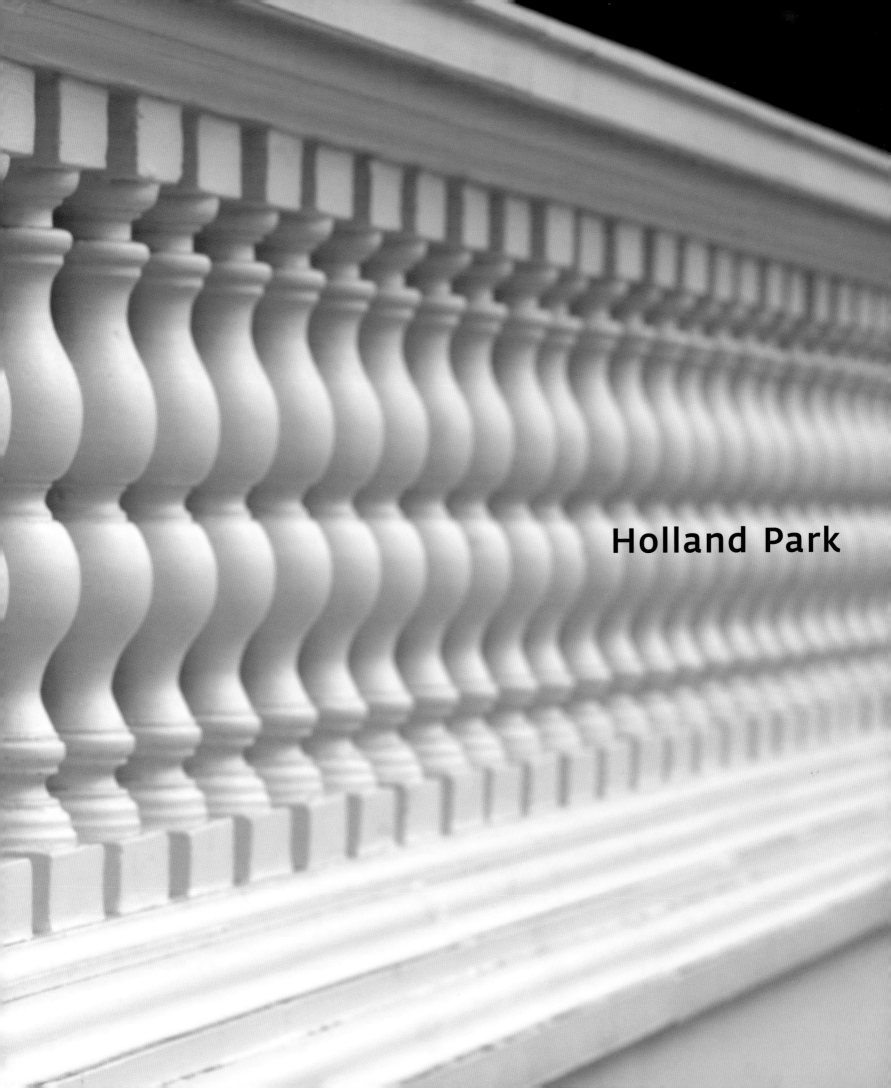

Holland Park

HOLLAND PARK

LONDON
2007

PRINCIPAL USE
Private residence

DESIGN
2005–2006

CONSTRUCTION
2006–2007.

GARDEN AREA
175 sq. m (1900 sq. ft)

For the garden designer, often the most challenging sites are not the rolling acres of country garden with their complex habitats but rather the confined city spaces in which every detail can be seen at close quarters. Level changes, in particular, must be precisely managed, since the addition or removal of spoil can be costly and inconvenient.

This commission represented such a conundrum: the space contained a substantial level change and had been excavated for a basement swimming pool, creating what was in effect a roof garden. Tall boundary walls on either side contained the garden and, ironically, the main view from the house required substantial screening. The garden's breadth was in its favour, but its lack of depth was a great limitation.

In front of the house is a simple garden planted with specimen olives and using the black-and-white marble tiling typical of the location. The drama unfolded to the rear of the house, where the swimming pool was taking shape below the higher level of the garden. Two skylights provide light to the pool space below, which acts as a connecting room to the mews house to the rear, also part of the property. Somehow these lights had to be absorbed into the fabric of the garden above.

The client's passion was for art and the carefully considered display of various significant pieces, the jewel among which was a remarkable monolithic sculpture by Anish Kapoor, *Sky Dish in Black Marble*, still in storage after its purchase in Italy. The new garden was to be its setting. Luciano had been commissioned after his successful engagement nearby (see pp. 151–61), but, despite this evidence of trust in his abilities, felt a pressure to produce a successful solution. Logistically this was a very demanding project: to make a serene garden from a construction site.

The lower level, which runs directly out from the house, was relatively straightforward. The building's recessed side wing allowed Luciano to create a generous outdoor dining space; simple uplighting of the exterior walls created a dramatic evening backdrop; and a polished concrete fireplace in the side wall introduced warmth and flickering light. Here, embraced by the house itself, the client could enjoy a high level of privacy – a huge asset in such a densely populated city. The connection between house and garden is at its strongest physically here, although the interior furnishings and decorations link closely to the garden as a whole, with many mirrored or polished surfaces that capture and redistribute light.

Steps to the higher level are paved in the same smooth, pale limestone as the terrace, and under-lit to create a theatrical backdrop. The levels are echoed in lines of tightly clipped box that run along the sloping bed between the terrace and lawn levels, providing a wall of foliage when viewed from the house.

At the higher level there were two main problems to resolve. First was the fact that this part of the garden is clearly visible (although not accessible) from the raised-ground-floor reception rooms, and needs to be successful when seen from there. Secondly, within this raised area the client still required privacy for a seating area and a lawn.

The rear planting had to be tall and preferably dynamic, full of movement and drama, in a move away from more static architectural hedging. Luciano selected black bamboo, *Phyllostachys nigra*, in part for its ebony stems but also for its height – he had found 12-metre (39 ft) specimens in a nursery in Italy – and elegance. The plants were craned into position, being too large to pass through the house itself, and they immediately gave life and movement to the garden, swaying in the wind like a great curtain. Tall blocks of beech hedging frame the upper garden, softening the side walls with flickering texture. The surface of the glass skylights, reflective by day, comes into its own at night as the light from below ethereally grazes the bamboo.

At the end of the lawn stands Kapoor's massive black-granite sculpture, its quarry marks retained, evidence of the struggle to pull the stone from the earth. The front, however, is finely polished, with a reflective concave circle that turns the world on its head. The piece stands like a watchful magic eye, presiding benignly over the garden. From the ground floor of the house the sculpture is in clear view, sparkling with captured light especially after dark, when the garden itself comes alive, beckoning a closer liaison and first-hand exploration.

After some discussion it was decided that a simple bed of gravel would suffice for the sculpture's setting, balancing the smaller coffee table and seating terrace on the opposite side of the garden. From here the grandeur of the piece can be seen fully, providing a fitting end point for the journey through the garden, invoking awe in its scale and mystery through its inviting and tantalizing surfaces, and completing the conversation between art, garden, interior and architecture.

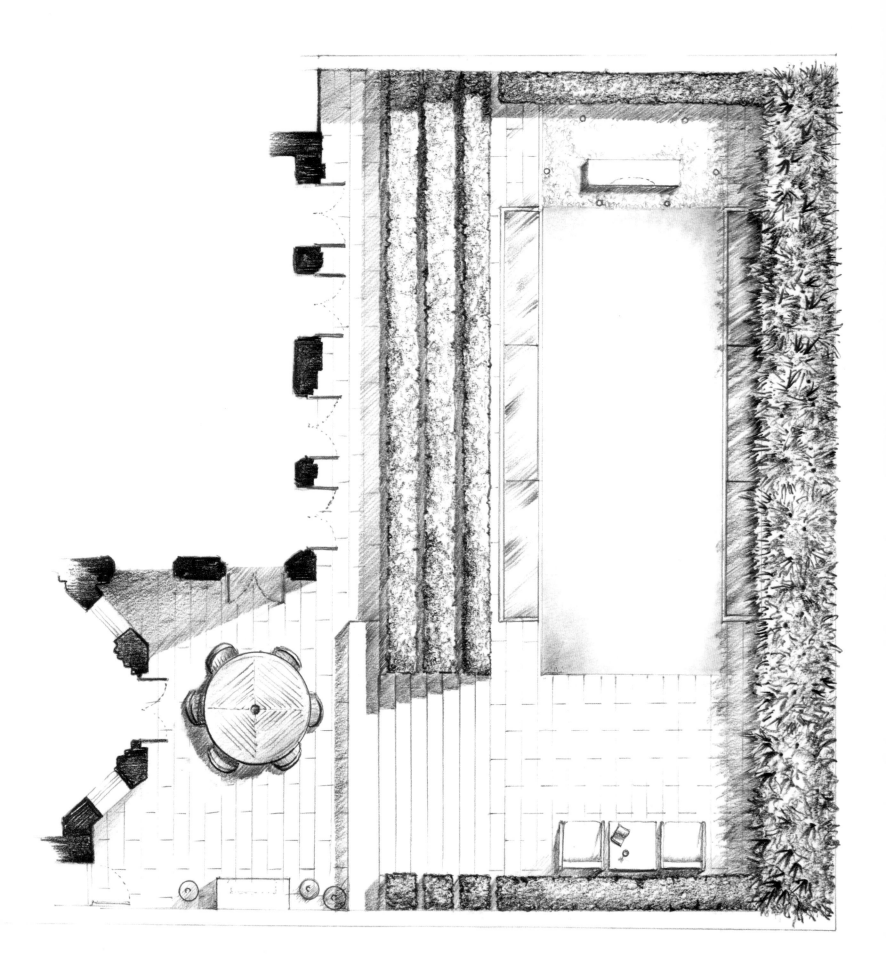

An overview (left) illustrates the problem of level change in this garden. From the lower floor (opposite) the views are upwards towards the bamboo screens, but from the raised ground floor (below) the whole space is more clearly revealed.

*The transformation of this place
from a dark hole to a glittering
stage for a magnificent sculpture
still amazes me.*

Controlled lines of box reinforce the stepped rise to the higher level. Skylights create the impression of reflective pools flush with the lawn, and the monumental sculpture by Anish Kapoor presides over the space to dramatic effect.

Lighting adds drama and reinforces the textures of surface and planting. Under-step lighting (opposite) adds grandeur to the change of level, and woven cones made from natural fibres (below, left) create intricate patterns on the smooth, neutral paving nearest the house.

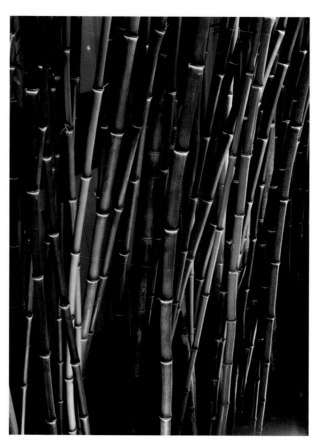

Collaborators

CONTRACTORS
Crocus
Guinness Pike
Jacquet
Landform Consultants
Landscape Associates
Massoni

NURSERIES
Bruns
Crocus
Rolando Innocenti & Figli
Lorberg Baumschulerzeugnisse
Lorenz von Ehren
Smits Tree Nurseries
Solitair
Van den Berk
M. van den Oever

ARTISTS AND CRAFTSMEN
Alan Hayward Joinery
Atelier Vierkant
B&D Design
Stephen Cox
Nathalie Decoster
English Hurdle
Nigel Hall
Hode Pottery
Alan Hughes
Anish Kapoor
Les Botta
Malcolm Martin and
    Gaynor Dowling
Matthew Collins Furniture
Paul Davies Design
Polidori Barbera Design
Read & Co.
Ahmed Sidki, BowWow
Keiichi Tahara

LIGHTING AND LIGHTING CONSULTANTS
Paul Cox
Delta Light
Jay Green
Tim Henderson, The Light
    Corporation
La Conch Lighting
Stanton & Brian Lighting
Wever & Ducré

WATER FEATURES
Andrew Ewing Aquatecture

IRRIGATION
Irrigation Projects &
    Management
Waterwell

STONE SUPPLIERS
CED
CITCO
Granite & Marble International

FURNISHINGS
B&B Italia
D Decor (Doreen Scott)
Dedon
Domani
Leisure Plan
Manutti
The Modern Garden Company
Summit Furniture
David Sutherland

ARCHITECTS AND INTERIOR DESIGNERS
ACQ Architects
Barrett Lloyd Davis Associates
Bill Bennette Design
Codecsa Constructora
Collett – Zarzycki
De Matos Ryan
Raoul Frauenfelder
Daniel Grataloup
Gilly Holloway
Kelly Hoppen Interiors
Mena Interiors
Michael Reeves Interiors
Graham Pockett
Ris Chabloz
Zanna Westgate
Joanna Wood

FLORISTS
John Carter Flowers
Paul Thomas Flowers

LUCIANO GIUBBILEI GARDEN DESIGN TEAM PAST AND PRESENT
James Aldridge
William Beresford
Jane Campbell
John Cavalheiro
Hiromi & David Kurita May
Catherine Macdonald
Melanie Reynard
Charlotte Sanderson
Jonathan Uglow

EDITORIAL SUPPORT
Susan Crewe
House & Garden
Clare Foster
House & Garden
Patrizia Gatti
Vogue Italia
Stephen Lacey
The Telegraph
Franco Marchesi
Elle Decor Italia
Juliet Roberts
Gardens Illustrated
Elspeth Thompson
The Telegraph

Index

ACKNOWLEDGEMENTS

I should first of all like to thank my clients, who have allowed me into their homes to photograph the finished gardens; without their generous support this book would not have been possible. I send my deepest appreciation to all the people who have worked with me: Melanie Reynard for her invaluable support; John Cavalheiro for beautiful drawings; and all the other members of my team – Catherine, Charlotte, David, Hiromi, James, Jane, Jonathan and William – for helping to run the projects.

I have been fortunate to have the opportunity to work with great contractors and specialists. Thank you to Mark Gregory, Richard Curle and Mark Fane for sharing my vision and enthusiasm; Andrew Ewing, who makes water look so effortlessly delicate; Andrew Wilson for writing so wonderfully; Steven Wooster for his patience in working with me and for seeing what I see; and the talented Alan Hughes for producing extraordinary drawings. I am grateful also to Balthazar Korab, who awakened my passion for photography and inspired me to design gardens the way I do; Tom Stuart-Smith, who has offered support and trust for which I shall always be grateful; and Peter Murray, who has shared my passion for art.

LUCIANO GIUBBILEI

Although we have remained great friends since Luciano first graduated, it has been a particularly enjoyable experience to work closely with him again, and I am grateful that he felt it appropriate for me to write this book. Our conversations and interviews were always memorable and fascinating, helped by good coffee and a shared love of classical music, which provided the soundtrack. Melanie Reynard from Luciano's office was a steady support to the project and deserves special gratitude.

I thank my wife, Barbara, and daughters, Rebecca and Naomi, who always forgave my departures into my office to complete the writing. Nigel Hall, Stephen Cox, Keiichi Tahara, Willy Janssens and Nigel Chapman were all generous with their time, and their thoughtful responses to my questions were very much appreciated. Project editor Rosanna Lewis also deserves a special mention for her patience and clarity of thought throughout the editing process. Thank you all.

ANDREW WILSON

First published 2010 by Merrell Publishers Limited, London & New York'

Merrell Publishers Limited
70 Cowcross Street
London EC1M 6EJ

merrellpublishers.com

Text and illustrations copyright © 2010 Luciano Giubbilei Limited, except where otherwise stated (see right)
Design and layout copyright © 2010 Merrell Publishers Limited

British Library Cataloguing-in-Publication data:
Wilson, Andrew, 1959–
The gardens of Luciano Giubbilei.
1. Giubbilei, Luciano. 2. Gardens – Design – Case studies.
I. Title II. Wooster, Steven.
712.6'092-dc22

ISBN 978-1-85894-644-3

Produced by Merrell Publishers Limited
Designed by Nicola Bailey
Project-managed by Rosanna Lewis

Printed and bound in China

PICTURE CREDITS

All images by Steven Wooster and © 2010 Luciano Giubbilei Limited, unless listed below.
TR = top right

Helen Fickling: 176–77, 187, 189; Foto Gielle: 12; Jerry Harpur: 15; Marcus Harpur: 183tr, 185; Florian Holzherr: 17; Alan Hughes: 22, 23, 31, 45, 59, 73, 101, 117, 137, 153, 179, 195, 209, 225; Balthazar Korab: endpapers, 10–11; Luciano Giubbilei Limited: 24–26; Keiichi Tahara: 94–97; VIEW/Richard Glover: 19; Jonty Wilde: 16; Herbert Ypma: 18.

JACKET, FRONT
Addison Road, London
see pp. 134–49

JACKET, BACK, PP. 8 & 238–39
Morocco
see pp. 114–33

FRONTISPIECE
Addison Crescent, London
see pp. 99–113

PAGES 6–7
The Boltons, London
see pp. 29–41